STAND WITH YOUR ARMOR ON

ANTHOLOGY OF DAILY CONFLICTS

CARIN JAYNE CASEY

STAND WITH YOUR ARMOR ON

Casey, Carin Jayne. *STAND With Your Armor On: Anthology of Daily Conflicts*

Copyright © 2021 by Carin Jayne Casey

Published by KWE Publishing: www.kwepub.com

ISBN (paperback): 978-1-950306-86-2 (ebook): 978-1-950306-87-9

Library of Congress Control Number: 2021908932

Unless otherwise noted, scripture in this book taken from the Authorized King James Bible. (Published by the World Publishing Company, New York.) New International Version (NIV) Holy Bible, New International Version ® NIV ® Copyright © 1973, 1978, 1984, 2011 by Biblica, Inc. ® Used by permission. All rights reserved worldwide.

Casey, Carin Jayne: STAND With Your Armor On: Anthology of Daily Conflicts 1. Christian Living - Social Issues 2. Christian Fiction -Contemporary 3. Body, Mind and Spirit - Healing - Prayers & Spiritual

NATIONAL DOMESTIC VIOLENCE HOTLINE

1-800-799-7233 or (TTY) 1-800-787-3224

ACKNOWLEDGMENTS

To my husband, family, siblings, and close friends go my sincere appreciation for believing in me, and for continually proffering me with your patience, positive support, and understanding. Always, I felt the Lord's inspiration, guidance, and grace during this writing adventure; for that, I am profoundly grateful. As I approach completion of this adventure, you may be wondering whether there are more books for me to write. I ask that same question to the Lord, "Will You bring me inspiration for another book?"

I am blessed with several awesome friends who are consistently supportive, whether in a business sense or spiritually; all encourage success within my calling. Those who immediately come to mind include: Vangie Hendrickson, Nayeli Cardona, Yolanda Gray, Angela B. Brown, Sharvette Mitchell, Tina Husk, Kamen Gordon, Amy Garelick, Kristin Spiers, Mary O. Moss, Catherine Arnold Brennan, and William Lightfoot. I sincerely appreciate each of you.

Specifically, I am grateful for the awesome kindness and support– especially patience, throughout my writings by my publisher and friend, Kim Wells Eley of KWE Publishing. And, many accolades for her expertise, generous guidance, and for pointing me to excellent resources, all to enable this story to come to life. We have successfully worked together to publish my previous book, *A New Song Rises Up! Sharing Struggles Toward Salvation*, and the complementary *Study Guide,* and now this book you have before you. I look forward to continuing our work together in future adventures.

PRAISE FOR "STAND WITH YOUR ARMOR ON"

From Catherine Brennan, award-winning author (Virginia Writer's Club Golden NIB Contest)

"**In this ugly and evil world,** we live in, Carin Casey's Anthology, **STAND With Your Armor On,** is both timely and appropriate. All too often, humankind turns to its own ways to solve its problems. If we first put on the whole armor of God, we are so much better off as our loving Father has nothing but good things for us.

Each of these powerful stories demonstrates what happens in the ugly world of sin—and yes, it is its own world—and they go on to show us how good God is.

These are not fairy tales but true-to-life stories with honest and accurate solutions. Carin has outdone herself."

From Yolanda Gray, LifeCoach.Author.Speaker

"**Here we have five short stories** that take you on a real-life journey into the intimate lives of people caught up in conflict, crime, and abuse. We see how they react to distressing situations and to the ultimate showdown of choice each one must make. Casey has developed each character—whether a victim or abuser—with such clarity and intensity. If you have ever been in any of the five situations described here, you will resonate with their dilemmas.

The themes of putting on the full armor (Ephesians 6:10) and the Biblical principal of sowing and reaping (Galatians 6:7-9) is clearly drawn in each story. Casey is a masterful storyteller. She gives you things to ponder throughout each story. Do you suit up, put on the armor of God, and follow Him or do you stay in the darkness and eventually end up reaping what you sow? This book works convincingly to give you the answer."

From Mary O. Moss – Founder and CEO of Divinely Designed, LLC, Linktr.ee/themarymoss

"**Five stories**, 1 common thread! The scenarios in this book are set up so that the reader can easily become 'part of the story.' The lessons provided in each episode are not lost on the reader: Rely upon our faith; use scripture as a guidebook. Choose to do what is right; repent when we don't chose wisely. Don't allow ourselves to be trapped by our circumstances. There are resources available for any situation in which we find ourselves. Sometimes we need to reach out to others for help. That is not a sign of weakness, but rather courage.

Carin Jayne Casey offers practical, actionable solutions to problems. She sets up questions for further thought and shares valuable information about resources available to anyone who may find themselves in a difficult, painful, complicated situation! I know reader's lives will be redeemed through reading this book! Read it yourself and share it with someone you believe can benefit!"

CONTENTS

INTRODUCTION

We all face worldwide evil; with it comes sickness, economic hardship, loss of loved ones, heartbreak, suffering, anger, and increased crime and political unrest.

Regardless, have you experienced amazing deliverance from hardships and pain that can only be explained by the awesome power of a good and just God?

If you can believe in a loving, merciful God, then you must know an evil, demonic force also exists. This evil is fighting to bring you nothing but pain, sorrow, chaos, and destruction.

Can you sense it all around you? A spiritual battle ensues, with light and darkness fighting for your soul!

Within each day may be horrible consequences or an overflow of abundance. Are you helpless to the outcome? Jesus explains this on-going spiritual conflict in John 10:10, The Passion Translation (TPT):

A thief has only one thing in mind—he wants to steal, slaughter, and destroy. But I have come to *give you everything in abundance, more than you expect*—life in its fullness until you overflow!

Hope is within your grasp, when you stand wearing the armor of God...

Have you experienced it? Have you fallen victim to acts of violence or rage, bringing you down? What about temptations that brought you to big mistakes that are followed by horrendous consequences?

I come from a lifetime of both good and bad things happening to me within the same timeframes. Chaos and conflicts abound while significant moments of peace miraculously came. In that, I am aware that there is a spiritual battle going on, a conflict—a fight for my peace, for my very life. How many of you can relate?

Some people will view themselves in life as a little balloon to be randomly tossed about, thrown in all directions, or crushed—all with no control over the direction they may travel or land. They lack control over thoughts that seemingly randomly come to them. But we are not little balloons; we are not mere animals. We each have a mind, heart, and soul. We have free will; and in that, we can and do make decisions.

Some people believe themselves self-sufficient: that they are ultimately in control, the master of their own fate. But at some point, each will learn the length and depth of their own steam and that power has insurmountable limits. None of us really know what tomorrow will bring; we don't even know whether we have just drawn our last breath.

For those of us who believe that the Lord God Almighty who created Heaven and earth and all living things is the ultimate power over our lives, we can decide to run to Him, and take solace.

The Word of God tells us in Genesis about the Fall of Mankind, when Adam and Eve listened to the enemy of God, the Devil, and disobeyed God's command. Even before that, the enemy had been an angel in Heaven, but had become so self-involved as to think he could overthrow our Creator.

Banished from Heaven, the Devil's desire is to take as many people down with him as he can, knowing that his day of reckoning, his severe judgment, is coming.

I am not a little balloon. I can see within my struggles where I have had the opportunity to choose my behavior and responses to the confusing and conflicting environment around me. My choices, whether to press for a better path or to return evil for evil, influenced the outcome in my future.

Isn't that true for us all? With every incident, regardless of the known and unknown influences and the temptations or encouragement surrounding us, we decide whether to sow into it love and goodness, or to sow revenge and offense.

We cannot escape the spiritual law of sowing and reaping. We decide for ourselves whether we sow good into our lives or evil. What we reap in the long run will coincide with our daily decisions sown; our consequences can be devastating and severe. Through it all, everything that happens in our lives can be utilized as learning tools for our growth.

We are encouraged by the Apostle Paul in Ephesians 6:10-18, New International Version, NIV, to put on the full armor of God as we face spiritual battles:

"Finally, be strong in the Lord and in His mighty power. Put on the full armor of God, so that you can take your stand against the devil's schemes. For our struggle is not against flesh and blood, but against the rulers, against the authorities, against the powers of this dark world and against the spiritual forces of evil in the heavenly realms."

Therefore put on the full armor of God, so that when the day of evil comes, you may be able to stand your ground, and after you have done everything, to stand.

Stand firm then, with the belt of truth buckled around your waist, with the breastplate of righteousness in place, and with your feet fitted with the readiness that comes from the gospel of peace. In addition to all this, take up the shield of faith, with which you can extinguish all the flaming arrows of the evil one. Take the helmet of salvation and the sword of the Spirit, which is the word of God.

And pray in the Spirit on all occasions with all kinds of prayers and requests. With this in mind, be alert and always keep on praying for all the Lord's people."

I always like to include the Christians' enthusiasm, or the cloak of zeal, as part of the armor we put on, which is described in Isaiah 59:17, New International Version (NIV), when the soldier "...wrapped himself in zeal as in a cloak."

I also encourage you to study the many scriptures that refer to the spiritual law of sowing and reaping, such as, Galatians 6:7-10, in the New Living Translation (NIV):

> "Don't be misled—you cannot mock the justice of God. You will always harvest what you plant. Those who live only to satisfy their own sinful nature will harvest decay and death from that sinful nature. But those who live to please the Spirit will harvest everlasting life from the Spirit. So let's not get tired of doing what is good. At just the right time we will reap a harvest of blessing if we don't give up. Therefore, whenever we have the opportunity, we should do good to everyone—especially to those in the family of faith."

I love to share a quote by D.L. Moody when I talk about this spiritual law:

> "The evil harvest of sin and the good harvest of righteousness are as sure to follow the sowing as the harvest of wheat and barley. Life is not casual, but causal."

We know our Heavenly Father's everlasting love for us because of the ultimate sacrifice He made so we can hope for a future. What was that sacrifice? Scriptures tell us, as in John 3:16, that Jesus is the only begotten Son of God, who suffered and died on the cross to pay for our sins; and He arose, defeating death (please refer also to Romans 10:9-10, John 14:6, and Acts 4:11-12). The Old Testament gives historic accounts of over three hundred prophecies which were miraculously fulfilled with the birth, crucifixion, and resurrection of Jesus Christ.

In reflection of such an unconditional love and grace from our Heavenly Father given us through Jesus Christ, my word for 2021 is *focus*. Focus on the Lord and His Kingdom and not on the distractions of this world. The world promises chaos, suffering, evilness, and destruction, while the Lord promises to bring peace and joy. What can I do? Run my race, fulfill my calling with my focus remaining on Jesus. What is the reward? As in Isaiah 26:3, New King James Version (NKJV): "You will keep *him* in perfect peace, *Whose* mind *is* stayed *on You,* Because he trusts in You."

The Lord brings promise and encouragement in many passages; for example, Joshua 1:9, New International Version (NIV): "Have I not commanded you? Be strong and courageous. Do not be afraid; do not be discouraged, for the Lord your God will be with you wherever you go."

There is hope for peace and prosperity when we turn to the Lord and hold fast to Him, as found in Deuteronomy 30:11-20. We have the individual choice, the free will, to choose a pathway toward life and blessings or toward death and curses.

I can admit that although I may have experienced heavy influences, I had free will; I was solely responsible for the bad choices I made along my journey. Often, the resulting consequences matched the gravity of those bad choices. How about you?

But also, I continue to face unsavory happenings that I had no choice over; in that, I'm responsible for my attitude. I can hope to respond with compassion and humility, knowing that God is my vindicator and that He is justice. I can overcome evil with good, as in Romans 12:19-21.

What if my answers to prayers seem to be long overdue? I can choose patient faith, as in Daniel 10:1-14, knowing that the Lord heard my prayers, but His angels may need to take time fighting through a spiritual battle to get to me. I can choose to sit in the heaviness of the ashes, or I can decide to exchange my mourning for beauty, the oil of joy, and the garment of praise, as in Isaiah 61:3.

Regardless how evil or harm comes to us, Scripture speaks about an attitude to maintain while we gravitate that unpleasant journey; such as, Romans 5:2-3, Amplified Bible (AMP):

> "Through Him we also have access by faith into this [remarkable state of] grace in which we [firmly and safely and securely] stand. Let us rejoice in our hope *and* the confident assurance of [experiencing and enjoying] the glory of [our great] God [the manifestation of His excellence and power]. And not only *this*, but [with joy] let us exult in our sufferings *and* rejoice in our hardships, knowing that hardship (distress, pressure, trouble) produces patient endurance..."

In that, the Lord promises troubles will not be more than we can bear, our situation is temporary, He is with us, and with Him we will have a means of escape (refer to 1 Corinthians 10:13). We can put on our armor and stand, as described in Ephesians 6, which requires personal action.

Did you mess up? Are you convicted of sin? There is a remedy: Sincerely turn to the Lord with repentance, accept Jesus as your Lord and Savior, and receive redemption (refer to for example Acts 2:38, Acts 4:12, John 14:6, Ephesians 2:8-9). Those who love Jesus have hope for a peaceful future! Jesus explains in John 16:33, New International Version (NIV) "...In this world you will have trouble. But take heart! I have overcome the world."

A Jesus-follower's path is clear: always hold your thoughts captive (2 Corinthians 10:3-5) as you let your own light shine (Matthew 5:15-16); share the good news with others (Mark 16:15) and plead for their salvation as an ambassador for Christ (2 Corinthians 5:18-20).

"Most of all, love each other as if your life depends on it. Love makes up for practically anything," according to 1 Peter 4:8, The Message (MSG). In Jesus, you have confidence that He hears you, your eternity is set, and no one can snatch you from Him (John 10:27-29).

You might say, "I pray. I read the Bible. I have memorized a few scriptures. Am I then prepared for spiritual battle, knowing, as in Ephesians 6:17, that the Word of God is my weapon? How important is it in today's world?"

Let us back up to Ephesians 6 again. The only weapon the soldier went to battle with was the sword of the Spirit. In 2 Corinthians 10:4, Amplified Bible (AMP),

> "The weapons of our warfare are not physical [weapons of flesh and blood]. Our weapons are divinely powerful for the destruction of fortresses."

Divinely powerful! What weapons? To prayerfully stand with the Word of God, as we noted earlier, is to hold the sword of the Spirit. Let me share a few passages in The Passion Translation (TPT) relating to the Word of God and how important to know and to live the Word of God is in your life.

Hebrews 4:12: "For we have the living Word of God, which is full of energy, like a two-mouthed sword. It will even penetrate to the very core of our being where soul and spirit, bone and marrow meet! It interprets and reveals the true thoughts and secret motives of our hearts."

2 Timothy 3:16 explains, "God has transmitted his very substance into every Scripture, for it is God-breathed. It will empower you by

its instruction and correction, giving you the strength to take the right direction and lead you deeper into the path of godliness."

John 1:1-4 (emphasis added), referred to as Christ, the Eternal Word: "In the beginning, the Word already existed. The Word was with God, and the Word was God. He existed in the beginning with God. God created everything through Him and nothing was created except through Him. The Word gave life to everything that was created, and His life brought light to everyone."

If you were to summarize the scriptures about the armor of God as according to what a soldier would wear in the day and time of the New Testament, it may briefly include these:

- Helmet of Salvation: A redeemed life and mindset as a follower of Jesus Christ;
- Breastplate of Righteousness: Gratefully walking obediently (in right living);
- Belt of Truth: God's Word is the ultimate truth, the light;
- Feet Shod with the Gospel of Peace: Peace of God in our lives with thankfulness;
- Shield of Faith: Focus on God's Kingdom rather than things of this earth;
- Sword of the Spirit: It is the Word of God, our weapon against the enemy; and
- Cloak of Zeal: Be zealous, enthusiastic for the Lord and for His calling in your life.

There are many good books and commentaries regarding the full armor of God, and I encourage you to make a study of it, so you will be well equipped in times of challenge. One of my favorites books is *The Armor of God* by Priscilla Shirer.

You may ask, "What does this armor during the New Testament days have to do with our daily conflicts and choices in our lives now?" and, "where and how does the armor of God fit in?"

In real life, we don't see the armor a person wears or their sword. That's why I chose to use the umbrella on the book cover. According to Wikipedia, the umbrella, parasol, or folding canopy is designed to shield or protect a person against rain or sunlight exposure.

For the device to be useful, the person must be prepared before facing harsh weather conditions by having it with them. But possession is not enough. They must open and hold up the umbrella at the appropriate time to hope for protection. We each choose whether to be prepared or not.

Similarly, God lovingly avails Himself to us for protection throughout life. But we decide to wear the armor of God or not. We choose if we will wield the weapon, the Word of God, or not.

Having possession of the Bible to read or as a decoration on the table is like having an umbrella in your closet. So when needed, we must be able to actively stand with our full armor on or face life's troubles without defense. Similarly, without your umbrella when needed, you might become soaked or sunburned.

My hope is that, as we read these stories together, the application of our armor within our daily conflicts will become more apparent.

PREFACE

If you have read prior books written by me or visited my podcast, *Turn to God with Carin*, then you can find common threads within my work. My desire is to bring you hope for healing and for a good future. Some key points are:

- We make decisions that either sow good for an eventual positive future, or they are evil choices that bring consequence. Sometimes, those consequences are horrific.
- We are now in the midst of a tremendous battleground between good and evil spiritual forces; the ultimate prize they each seek is our souls.
- There is hope and healing available to each of us when we turn to God seeking forgiveness, rescue, and salvation through Jesus Christ.

My personal testimony, shared in my previous book, *A New Song Rises Up!*, includes a life of abuse, much of it being life-threatening: child abuse, domestic violence, and abuse within a toxic environment. While at my lowest point in the pit of despair, I cried out to the Lord for forgiveness, rescue, and salvation through Jesus Christ. Although I did not deserve it, He delivered me. I am a domestic violence victim advocate and ambassador for Christ.

My gratitude motivates me to encourage you, my dear reader, to turn to the Lord with whatever challenges you may face. If I can be redeemed through Jesus Christ, you can, too!

As I wrote *A New Song Rises Up!*, I addressed more deeply the spiritual warfare we face and the concept of putting on the full armor of God. You can find this information in the chapter titled *"Are You Experiencing Spiritual Warfare?"*

But in layman's terms, do we really have a full realization of the battles that are going on right now and all around us?

You may sense through sight, sound, and emotions the unsavory arguments, conflicts, and attacks happening. But do you understand how your very thoughts might be insidiously infected and bombarded by innuendo, blatant suggestions, and lies?

Stand With Your Armor On is an anthology solely by **Carin Jayne Casey** of five separate and fictional stories. Each story has its own individual characters, cast, and setting featured; some stories capture short periods of time while others span over many years. Tales within these pages are meant to present readers with realistic scenarios in our world today and to encourage an eye-opening experience.

These five fictional stories are shared with sincere hopes of helping others. I cannot escape the inclusion of my personal interpretations and perceptions of life. Nothing I write is intended to depict any particular individual or to cause any harm. As an American, I enjoy the freedom to express my thoughts, opinions, and position regarding any ongoing issues in today's society. As a Christian, I encourage each person to do this: if God has brought you through something and provided you His miracles, then tell others in whatever way you can.

Stand With Your Armor On is my attempt to broaden our awareness of the influences we may face, as well as the potential lasting effects. These stories contain cautionary tales of potential temptations, which may be through family, friends, the environment we live in, or even ourselves. If we choose to respond with evil thoughts, intentions, words, and actions, then consequences will follow. But also, we find there is forgiveness, restoration, and redemption offered through the Lord Jesus Christ. In Him, we can put on the full armor of God and withstand enemy attacks and temptations that come.

Ultimately, I hope you will decide that it is imperative to always *Stand With Your Armor On*!

Enjoy your reading adventure!

ONE

WHO IS DIRECTING YOUR STEPS?
EFFECTS OF AN ANGRY, PRIDEFUL HEART

In this story, we have a father, Brian, and his young adult son, Marcus, a high-school graduate with plans for college in the fall. They live together in an affluent neighborhood, somewhere in suburbia, USA. Brian is a well-respected member of the local Baptist church. He has established a thriving, successful business while raising Marcus as a single parent. Brian acts on the board of directors for a local non-profit organization, and currently finances an excellent college career path for Marcus. What could possibly go wrong?

After making sure that no one was tailing him, Marcus quickly parked his car in an inconspicuously dark area in the backyard of his father's home. He felt confident that even when the sun rose it would remain hidden under the old willow tree.

Still shaking, Marcus grabbed the soiled rags from the passenger seat; he had used them just an hour ago to mop up the blood. *So much blood!* He glanced at the rags and almost allowed himself to engage in remorse, but he flashed back to what had just happened and his anger reignited. *Stupid bitch! Why did she have to diss me like that?*

From the car, Marcus rushed to the back door. *Locked!* He ran around to the front door and tried it, finding that door also locked. He searched for the key, believing it would be in the same place his father always hid it, under a rock behind the front bushes. *Got it!*

Quickly, he opened the door, typed in the security code to stop the house alarm, and ran into his father's bedroom, throwing the French doors wide open.

"Dad, Dad, wake up!" Marcus shook his father's shoulder and flicked on the light at the nightstand.

Confused, his father rubbed his eyes and mumbled, "What is it? What's going on?"

Marcus sat in the chair beside the bed, saying, "Dad, I need you to wake up and help me." He clasped his hands together to keep them steady. "I'm in trouble ..."

Brian sat up in the bed and stared at his son, who was obviously scared and upset about something. "Son, whatever it is you've gotten yourself into, I can handle it." Confidently, he continued, "Calm down and tell me what your problem is."

Marcus licked his lips, saying, "Dad, you were right about Dolores, she wasn't good enough for me, she wasn't worth my time." He glanced around the room. "She only caused me trouble."

"Just what I thought, son," Brian shook his head, glad that Marcus finally acknowledged the truth about her. Brian considered himself to be wise and discerning when it came to his son.

Yes, they had only dated a short while, but Marcus' time was too important, too precious to be wasted on someone who was obviously beneath him. Every moment spent with her could potentially rob him of opportunities for his successful future.

"What did she do?"

"Well. You see, well, um, we were with my friends at O'Malley's earlier this evening, having a few drinks, and we started joking around. You know, like we do." He leaned in. "Dolores was a big pain the whole time. I tried to ignore her. She kept tugging at me and whispering that she wanted to leave. Finally, I had enough of her crap and squeezed her arm tight. I said, loud enough for my friends to hear, 'Shut up! If you don't like it, go sit somewhere else. But leave me the hell alone!'"

As Marcus told his story, his dad looked at the bloody rags on his son's lap, and he noticed the blood still on his hands. He grimaced and braced himself, afraid of what he might hear next.

Brian said, "Did she? Did she shut up and leave you alone?"

Marcus glared at the wall. "Hell no. She jumped up and shouted – loud enough for *everyone* at the bar to hear – 'Gladly! I'm sick of hanging around with you and your losers, anyway!' Then, she threw her drink in my face. Before I could react, she had already pranced out the door. Can you believe it? She threw her drink right in my face! It set me on fire! Dad, everyone, not just my so-called friends, but *everyone* in the place was laughing at me!

"And then her slutty little friend, Gina, said she was calling the cops, so I had better not hurt Dolores. That really burned me up."

Angry now himself, Brian moved his legs to the floor, exclaiming, "You didn't deserve that! How dare Dolores insult you – dishonor you publicly – like that!"

Marcus nodded in agreement and continued, "I rushed out after her, caught her by the arm in the parking lot and dragged her ass to my car. She fought me, but I forced her in. Then I raced to her crummy little apartment. We yelled at each other all the way. I was so angry! I was boiling mad!"

Encouraging Marcus and patting him on the shoulder, Brian said, "That stupid bitch!"

"Once we got there, she tried to shut the front door in my face. Imagine that! Here I was the one who paid her apartment rent last month!"

"What? Son...you paid her rent?"

Ignoring his dad's inquiry, Marcus continued, "But of course, I was able to shove my way through and slammed it closed. I pulled her to me so that her face was only inches from mine. I shouted, 'How *dare* you diss me like that in front of my friends!' and with my hands on her throat, I pushed her backwards real hard and smashed her head against the fireplace mantle."

Marcus held his breath for a moment, then gulped in air. He pushed himself to finish telling, while wringing his hands uncontrollably with the bloody rags on his lap.

"Dad, her eyes rolled back, and blood poured out of her head. I mean, it poured out..."

Marcus searched his father's expressions while a strange, partial memory flashed into his mind. The memory was not of what he had done, but of his father's angry and devilishly contorted face while he screamed with his hands clenched around Marcus' mother's throat, so many years ago. Marcus shook his head to free himself of the past. *Focus, man! You are losing it!*

He gazed again at his father and barked, "I was in shock, Dad. I let go of her and she just fell limp onto the floor."

Both men held their breath with deafening silence permeating the air.

Finally, with earnest fear for his son, Brian asked, "Was she dead?"

Looking down at his bloody hands nervously, he responded, "Well...yeah. I didn't check, but how could anyone live with all that blood pouring out?"

Almost in a whisper, he attempted to explain. "Dad, I didn't mean for her to die. I did not, I did *not* realize she would hit the mantle, or hit it so hard... that was out of my control!"

A tear fell from Brian's eye as he reached over and patted his son on the shoulder, consoling him. In a soothing, calming voice, he said, "I know, son. It was not your fault. She brought this on herself." Enforcing his resolve, he announced more emphatically, "She should have known better than to disrespect you at all, especially in public." He placed his hand on Marcus' head as if to soothe his problems away, while they both quietly faced the horrors of the night.

Brian took out a handkerchief and wiped his face. "Son, what did you do next?" While fixing his gaze on the rags in Marcus' lap, he inquired, "I guess you tried to clean up the mess. Did you leave her there?"

Marcus began to cry. "Yeah, like I said, I was in shock. I tried to clean it up, but there was so much blood...I just had to get out. So I bolted out of there. At first, I drove around, not sure what I could do...Dad, I was so confused. All I could think of was to come home. I knew you would be able to handle this. I drove here and hid my car out back, under the willow tree."

"Did anyone see you with her in the parking lot? Did anyone see you at her apartment?"

Bewildered, Marcus could not remember looking around. At the time, his sole focus, his white-hot anger, had been on Dolores. "I don't know..."

Brian bit his tongue, considering the seriousness of the matter. He stood up from the bed and glanced at the clock. "It's just a matter of time before the police come knocking on the door. We've got to get ready."

He grabbed his pants from the other side of his bed and began putting his clothes on. Searching in his dresser, he found clean socks, then slid his loafers on, announcing, "I need to call my lawyer right now."

He glanced over at his son, who was still sitting in the chair. "Marcus! Get moving, *now*! Go take a shower and I'll burn those bloody rags."

Sheepishly, Marcus obeyed.

What have we learned so far about Brian and Marcus? Did we just get a glimpse into a past of domestic violence, witnessed by Marcus at a tender age? Does it seem that father and son may view themselves as better than others? What might Marcus be facing as consequence to his rash explosion of violence?

In the early morning hours, loud sirens and lights flashed from several police vehicles within the quiet community. All of the vehicles converged and parked at Brian's home. While a few officers surrounded the front and back doors, others easily found Marcus' car in the backyard.

While Marcus cowered in the bedroom, Brian quickly put his face mask on (to protect himself from potential exposure to a mutation of the worldwide COVID virus) and opened the door and announced, "I have contacted my attorney, who will be here within the hour. Meanwhile, Marcus will not speak with anyone," Brian said to an officer.

The officer in charge produced a warrant to search the premises, Marcus' belongings, and the vehicles at that property. The search began.

Although the rags had been set on fire in the fireplace, there were sufficient pieces remaining to submit to the lab. Marcus was swabbed for DNA, with the promise that fingerprints were to be secured at the station.

Frustrated at the way the police officers were rummaging throughout the house and then man-handling Marcus, Brian yelled, "Hey, hey, what do you think you're doing! My attorney is not here yet! You're touching everything—you're presenting me and my son with a health hazard!"

"Sir, please do not obstruct, stand aside. We have sufficient information to arrest this man," the lead officer said. He then nodded to another officer, barking, "Read him his rights."

Before Brian could say or do another thing, Marcus had already been charged, handcuffed, and was being hauled off to the station.

Marcus looked back at his father from the back of the squad car; in a moment of clarity, he envisioned the likelihood that his future was completely ruined. He knew this is only the beginning of a terrible ride down into his lowest depths of the pit. *I'm going straight to hell*, he thought to himself.

While Brian waited for his attorney to answer the cell phone, this proud man felt faint and grabbed the door facing. He watched them destroy his house from the doorway. He looked on helplessly while the officers tore every room of his home apart. Nothing he had was valued or considered sacred any longer. His emphatic objections to their treatment of his precious treasures were ignored. He could envision virus germs growing exponentially on every surface.

"I do not deserve this," Brian muttered under his breath.

Attorney Lewis Sheen answered his cell phone and heard Brian, who was frantic.

"Lewis, you've *got* to do something! They have already charged Marcus and hauled him off. Officers are still here, tearing my house apart! They are spreading virus germs all over my house!" He listened in despair, while his attorney explained typical requirements and procedures of a warrant. "Yes, I read it, the warrant includes all that." He sadly shook his head. "Yes, I understand."

He listened to his attorney's opinion regarding the officers' search within the home, that this could be resolved with a housekeeping crew. With anxiety only slightly lowered, he acknowledged,

"Yes, please do call a trustworthy cleaning team for the house. Tell them this is a health emergency, and their price is not a problem!" Brian reluctantly agreed, "Okay, we can meet at the precinct once they leave here."

After he hung up from talking with his attorney, he began to cry bitterly, something he had not allowed himself to do since his childhood. He pounds his fist on his ornate office desk, causing a precious antique sculpture to fall to the floor and break.

It is scary to realize how quickly our world can change on us within only moments of time – overnight. It only took Marcus one fit of rage, one act of violence...

Have you ever made a significant decision that ultimately changed the entire course of your life? Were you the one in control, or did you allow outside forces to influence or guide you?

∾

Once at the precinct, Marcus announced loudly, "I have an attorney. I'm not saying anything without him!"

An officer responded, "No problem. We're just getting you processed for now."

While being fingerprinted and getting his mugshots taken, Marcus remained distraught and confused, while he watched himself wringing his hands. *How did I get here, and so quickly?*

Although, he of course knew full well what he had done to get there. He would not allow himself to feel defeated. *No worries! Dad will get me out of this mess... somehow. He is a powerful man!*

While he sat in the little interrogation room alone, his mind felt as if it was wandering into a thick fog. He looked down at his hands and for only a brief second, he thought that he could still see her blood on them. Rubbing his hands vigorously together, he mumbled, as if to convince himself, *Man, you have got to keep it together! There is NO blood on your hands!*

The minutes passed at an unnervingly slow pace. With no clock and no window, he had no idea what time it was. For the first time since he arrived, Marcus looked around at his surroundings.

There was nothing in the little room other than a small table, his own chair, and an empty chair. He wondered how many other people had sat in this same room, this chair, and had had their hands on this table. *Would they bother to wipe this room down between interrogations?* He doubted it, and drew his hands to his chest.

He could hear people casually chatting and laughing outside of his door. With a burst of belligerence, he yelled, "Where is that damn lawyer?"

Immediately answering himself in self-pity, *I have been forgotten.*

It appears that Marcus is experiencing a variety of negative emotions while he struggles for some simulation of self-control to fight off his desperate fears with waning self-confidence, even with bouts of righteous indignation.

Have you ever found yourself in such a horrific quandary that brought on a whole gambit of mixed feelings and emotions all at once?

What could have helped him in this moment of despair?

We can always turn to the Lord, pray for His rescue in any circumstance. As in Psalm 46:1, KJV (King James Version), "God is our refuge and strength, a very present help in trouble."

Attorney Lewis Sheen met with Brian outside of the police precinct. As they shook hands Brian greeted him with a burst of relief.

"Hey Lewis, I'm so glad to see you. Boy, oh boy! Do I have a problem for you to solve this time!"

Lewis calmly patted Brian on the shoulder. "No reason to worry yet, my friend. We just need to assess this situation."

Lewis gestured for Brian to enter the open door to the back seat of his car with him so they could speak privately before entering the precinct.

Once they were both settled into the back of his Cadillac sedan, Lewis again explained why it was more expedient to meet here instead of at the house, especially since Marcus was already at the precinct. He encouraged Brian to tell him everything he knew, including every known detail.

Anxiously, Brian proceeded with all that he had been told by Marcus, and all he had observed. Finishing his tale with the upset of officers tearing his house and his son's car all to pieces, Brian exclaimed, "I just can't believe this has happened and my son is facing charges. If only Marcus had listened to me, none of this would have happened. I knew that girl was nothing but trouble!"

Lewis looked at his pad and scribbled some notes. "Brian, I guess we can assume everyone in the bar saw and heard Marcus and Dolores arguing, and her friend threatening to call the police. Then he angrily followed Dolores out the door. Even if no one saw him force her into his car or into her apartment, there may have been witnesses or strong circumstantial evidence of that happening. You know, DNA, fingerprints, damage to the front door, and so on."

He adjusted his glasses before he continued. "By the way, when I was informed about the warrant, I was also told that there was a witness at Dolores' apartment who had called the police."

He paused, waiting for that information to sink in, and then continued, "So we don't have much to say about that evening other than the truth..."

Lewis studied Brian, who remained deep in thought. Brian was constantly rubbing his temples in hopes to relieve the overwhelming pressure inside.

Even though there did not appear to be much wiggle room as far as the facts of the matter, Lewis entertained potential scenarios as defense.

"Once inside the apartment, who knows? Maybe she attacked him first, threatened him with something, or at least there was a mutual struggle. A crime of passion, an uncontrollable emotional outburst of anger and rage, with no plan to harm her, no intentions of it going that far..."

He stopped and looked at his friend. Brian was trying to conceal that he was wiping away tears. Lewis had never seen him without complete control and composure. That is, before this incident.

Lewis studied his notes that he had jotted down thus far.

"I'm interested in what the coroner's report has to say. Brian, what did they find during their search of the house and his car?"

Sheepishly, Brian scratched his head, admitting, "I don't know what might have been in the car, other than blood. He still had blood on his hands when he woke me up. I had instructed him to go wash and take a shower while I attempted to burn the bloody rags in our fireplace. But unfortunately, they found little pieces of those bloody rags during the search."

Lewis interrupted Brian, asking, "Did you say anything to them about that?"

Immediately, Brian sat up and straightened his shoulders. "Oh no, I knew not to tell them anything without an attorney's presence."

Almost as quickly, he was overcome with great concern for himself, and asked, "Did I just bring myself into the crime when I tried to burn those rags? Am I in trouble, too? Am I now an accessory-after-the-fact...to murder?" He could feel his heart clinch.

Lewis gave his friend a gentle pat on the shoulder, "Let us not get ahead of ourselves, that may become a non-issue... don't concern yourself with it right now. But, if you feel like you are ready, I think we had better go into the precinct now. Is that okay with you?"

Sadly, Brian mumbled, "Sure. Let's face the music."

What do you think might happen to Marcus? Do you think Brian may face charges as well? After all, he did try to destroy evidence...

The next step in our journey is the arraignment proceeding, where Marcus is formally advised of the charges against him and asked to enter a plea to those charges. If Marcus pleads not guilty, the prosecution must prove guilt in court.[1]

Marcus pled not guilty.

~

Remand was demanded because the Judge had determined Marcus' father had means to create a flight risk, with Marcus' charges for first degree murder. Brian was thankful their state was not one to hold the death penalty. But as soon as he felt that relief, he imagined that just by being in prison with a worldwide virus running rampant in the prisons. *Wow, maybe just being there is a death sentence?* He tried to push those fears out of his mind.

"Marcus, don't worry, it's just for a short time," Brian tried to assure Marcus.

Attorney Sheen was not so optimistic, as he advised, "Just make sure you do what they say, and don't cause any trouble. No fighting! Any negative actions will not be looked upon lightly..."

Marcus was beside himself. Brought up with a 'silver spoon' hanging out his mouth, he was shocked to be placed in what he considered deplorable conditions. Realizing that he no longer had even his cell phone, Marcus was both indignant and fearful. *Oh, come on! Am I going to the same accommodations as a common criminal? Really?* Still not fully understanding his situation, he rallied himself, *Oh, no, my dad will not put up with that!*

Within moments of his arrival into his cell (his new home for God knew how long), his huge, muscular, and disgusting-looking room-mate said threateningly, "Let's get it straight from the start. Folks around here call me Killer. I'm not afraid of you, and if you mess with me, I'll kill you." Then he gave Marcus a sinister smile, showing yellowish brown teeth. "Hey, maybe I'll kill you anyway, just for the fun of it." He laughed as if he was insane.

Marcus had never before experienced the terror that now gripped his entire being. He remained petrified and stayed out of Killer's way the best he could, while residing in that tiny cell they shared. He looked around at the two tiny beds and toilet, shocked at such meager surroundings.

During their first hour of sleep in that 'hell-cell' together, Killer awoke and said sarcastically, "Hey, Marcus, come over here... I'm lonely, and I've got a nice surprise for 'ya..." Then Killer laughed loudly, adding, "Don't worry, whenever I have the need, I can find you."

Marcus laid wide-awake, frozen in place the entire night. *How many ways can I die here? Murdered? Diseased? Tortured 'til I wished I could die?*

From that night on, Marcus spent his nights only dozing for short intervals, always striving to listen for every movement, every snore, and even every breath from his roommate. One day in jail with Killer felt like a lifetime. While he was overwhelmed with fear, every moment was fragile.

Can you imagine the total change in Marcus' environment? Through his thoughts and words, culminating into the actions of one night, maybe one hour, has brought him from a life of luxury and control to horrific, life-threatening consequences. How can he survive it?

He is experiencing mental and emotional conflict: striving to rally himself while also terrified. Do you agree that even in the worst situations, we have choices as to where our thoughts take us?

2 Corinthians 10:5, TPT (The Passion Translation) tells us:

> *We can demolish every deceptive fantasy that opposes God and break through every arrogant attitude that is raised up in defiance of the true knowledge of God. We capture, like prisoners of war, every thought and insist that it bow in obedience to the Anointed One.*

∼

Although they had to wait nearly a year for the trial date, the trial itself was swift, as was the verdict. Marcus wondered, *Will I be here for the rest of my life? Will I even have a life after prison?* Nervously, he tried to control his fearful shaking.

The judge asked the jury's foreman, "How do you find the defendant on the charge of first- degree murder?"

The foreman answered, "Of the charge, first degree murder, we find the defendant not guilty."

The judge continued, "Of the charge, second degree murder, how do you find?"

Marcus looked down at the table in front of him, too afraid to look at the jury members. This was the charge his attorney had warned he likely would receive. He braced himself.

"Of the charge, second degree murder, we find the defendant guilty."

Marcus' ears began to ring so loudly that he couldn't hear what was said next. Attorney Lewis Sheen spoke to him, but he only under-stood his gestures for Marcus to follow the officers of the court. Marcus obediently followed, knowing sentencing would come later.

Darkness clung to his sunken eyes from living in continuous fear and sleep deprivation. Meals rarely agreed with him, leaving him emaciated. *How could it be any worse in my next prison cell?* he wondered.

Marcus looked up for a moment, thinking of saying a prayer, but he changed his mind, *No, God is not looking at me. I've been a stranger to Him for years. I deserve nothing.*

Admitting he now officially carries that title, he shouted in self-disgust, "I am a murderer!"

Sentencing came the next week. What happened in-between was a blur for him. However, Attorney Sheen did explain that second degree murder was "... punishable by confinement in a state correctional facility for not less than five nor more than forty years."[2]

Marcus had hoped his sentence would not be for the maximum. And it wasn't... but twenty-five years of prison life is a very long time. *This one year in jail had seemed like forever...I will be in my fifties before seeing freedom again! If I live through it...*

What did they say about chances for parole? He couldn't remember what they had said, but he thought they might have said there was a chance.

Does it matter? he wondered. He could not imagine surviving imprisonment even ten years.

Twenty-five years! After the year with Killer, is he going to live long enough to see, feel, and touch freedom ever again? But finally, we do see change in his attitude; that of shame, and maybe remorse...

Brian slowly sauntered into the small, congested visitors' room where there were a number of what looked like open telephone booths with a chair waiting at each. A security guard led him to an empty chair and told him to wait.

After several nerve-wrecking moments, Brian got his first glimpse of his son since he had been sentenced at the trial, six months ago.

Oh my God, he looks terrible! He's so skinny and pale. This will be harder than I thought!

Brian's eyes made a quick inspection of the room, as if he could spot virus germs gathering around him. He shuddered, believing himself placed in harm's way of the virus or other germs or diseases by coming into the prison facility to visit Marcus. He glanced around the area again, assuring himself, *At least, nobody I know will see me here. I can be thankful for that. It's bad enough I have to come into this facility myself.*

Marcus picked up his phone and smiled at his dad, giving Brian the cue to pick his phone up so they could hear each other through the glass.

"Hi Dad, I'm so glad you came!"

Marcus mustered up a cheerful appearance; he was sincerely thankful to finally get to see his dad after waiting for him to visit during these first few very long months in prison. Marcus wondered, *Where were you, Dad? I needed you!*

"Hello son, how are you?" Brian addressed Marcus with a strong, confident voice, but then he hesitated, shifting in the chair to make himself more comfortable. "I'm sorry I couldn't make it here earlier...I had so much going on at the office...well, you know how it is. And it takes me at least a couple of hours to get here."

"That's fine, Dad, I'm just glad to see you here now."

"How are they treating you? Are you getting enough to eat?" Brian leaned in with concern, asking, "Have you been sick? Are the other inmates leaving you alone?"

"Sure. All's fine. And I've been vaccinated."

Marcus told himself, *No point in goin' on about how scary it is here. Then Dad would surely think I was a coward.*

"Of course, it's taking me some time to get used to this change in my environment."

Brian responded quickly (maybe too quickly) while he glanced at the clock on the wall, saying, "That's great, son. I've been vaccinated, too." He shifted in his chair. "I knew you could handle it."

An awkward silence followed, with neither of them knowing what to say next. Marcus desperately wanted to ask, "*Dad! Why didn't you come to see me after the trial? Why have you left me waiting for you these six long months?*" But Marcus knew it would only serve to make his proud father upset, and maybe he would not come back at all. He decided not to ask.

Brian, now considering Marcus to be a blemish to the family, fought off the irritation that came from the absolute shame of having to come to this lowly depth to visit his now obvious loser of a son. Self-righteously he felt, *I do not deserve such humiliation! I did everything I could for this boy, sacrificed my time and money for his future...and now look at him!*

He resolved to be the better man who could hold up in the storm and to remain kind in this moment. He struggled to think of something, but he could not come up with anything to talk about. Brian looked at the clock again.

"Son, is there anything I can bring you next time? Do you get magazines here? Do you need toiletries or clothes?" Exasperated, he admitted, "I have no idea what I should bring you for the next visit. You will need to tell me what you might need."

Marcus smiled, pushing to respond positively, "I'm just glad to see you, Dad, you don't need to bring anything."

"What about your friends, have any of them come to visit?" Glancing at the clock again, Brian struggles with irregular breathing, thinking, *Time is not at all moving fast enough! I need to get out, get out, get out!*

Marcus looks down at his hands sadly, "No, they're probably too busy right now."

Carefully, Marcus considered whether he should mention that the prison pastor had befriended him. He decided it would take a load of worry off his dad if he knew someone on the inside cared.

"But lately, the prison pastor has been coming to see me pretty often." He added, "He's nondenominational so there's no worry that I'll be changing my beliefs, but it's nice to have someone to talk with."

Slightly irritated about a pastor talking with his son without his consent or control, Brian asked, "What kind of things does he have to talk with you about? Is he trying to cause you to become a Jesus freak?"

Sheepishly Marcus responded, "No, but he did ask me to share about my childhood. You know, my upbringing..."

"Oh." Brian's voice fell short. "So, he asked about your mother, did he?"

"He first wondered why she had not come to visit me. Then, he became interested in knowing the story behind her abandoning us, that's all."

Marcus looked into his father's eyes with unspoken questions. *Why did she leave us, Dad? Why did she really leave me?*

"The pastor asked where she might be now, and if she knows that I'm in prison... for a very long haul."

He paused, not sure that he should continue, before finally blurting out, "It would be nice if she knew where I am; maybe she could come visit. Who knows? Maybe it's possible she and I could start a relationship."

Immediately, Marcus regretted saying that. *Oh, God! Now he's going to blow up!*

Already feeling the rage building up inside him, Brian quipped, "Relationship? Really?"

He straightened himself in his chair and cleared his throat. "Well, don't look at me, I have no idea where she is or what she knows. She has been completely out of our lives all these years." He waved his arms in anger-fueled exasperation. "She could be anywhere. She could have remarried. I would not have a clue how to find her if I had to."

He tried to control the anger that was rising within, adding, "Besides, Marcus, have you forgotten? She abandoned you while you were still a young child. Why in the hell would you want to start a relationship with her?"

Marcus was having trouble controlling anger building in himself. Meanwhile, Brian bristled with offense that this pastor was delving into their personal family matters, as if he hadn't had enough suffering to deal with. Brian said crisply, "You can certainly tell your pastor to contact me. I can tell him more about that woman than he could ever want to hear." He added, "After all, you were only five years old when she left you, what can *you* hope to remember?"

Marcus forced courage within himself to say what he's been wanting to address for a long time. "I do remember the fights. I remember you were always mad and yelling at her. Sometimes, you were hitting or pushing her. She was always scared and crying."

Somehow Marcus felt empowered, as if he had finally been able to stand up for his mother, after all these years. *There. I have said my truth. Let the chips fall where they may...*

Brian exploded, shouting, "Oh my God! That is *not* how it was. I never did anything to that woman!"

Brian realized he had raised his voice and began to fight off the offense he suffered from what his son had just said. He thought, *I will try to let it slide just this once, but Marcus had better not speak of or accuse me of abuse again.*

Clearing his throat, Brian clarified, "Son, this is certainly not the right time for you to revisit sad times in your past. It can only bring you down." Looking at the clock one last time, he said as kindly as he could, "You were a young child. No wonder you don't remember it as it actually happened."

Marcus shook his head to contradict his father, staring directly into his eyes. *I know the truth, Dad. I know why Mom had to leave...she was scared to death of you!*

Brian fought to gain composure while also noticing the defiance in his son's demeanor, wagging his head in denial of what Brian had told him.

Brian then puffed his chest out and confidently explained, "Son. I want you to look at me carefully. You are looking at an honorable man. I have more integrity in my pinkie finger than any other person you may know, even if you compared me to your pastor friend. What I say is true."

Silently, he thought, *To hell with you, after all I have done for you, the sacrifices I've made for your sake...Well, you have lost any further support from me!*

Marcus looked down at his hands again, knowing he would never get the true story about that day his mother left. *He must have threatened her or forced her out. She probably was a great mother.* Marcus sighed heavily, thinking, *Dear God, please find my mother for me!*

Brian glared at his son for a few moments. *What the hell is he doing now? Praying? Oh, brother...*

Standing up, Brian announced, "Well, look at the time... I've got to go for now, but I'll be back... sometime." Awkwardly he waved his hand towards his son, but he couldn't bear to look Marcus in the eyes, "I love you, son... Take care."

He congratulated himself for giving a kind closing remark, which he considered very big for him to do under the circumstances. He returned to his superior posture as he began to walk away.

Marcus briefly pressed his hand to the glass while he watched his father walk away. "'Love you too, Dad." *I won't be seeing you again, will I?*

Brian held his stature so high that Marcus imagined his father's nose lifted to the heavens as he marched out of the room. Marcus watched for it, but his father did not look back.

Wow, this scene was a big reveal, wasn't it? Do you see where Marcus' confrontation for truth, although unpleasant, was instrumental for him in making a significant, pivotal change? Sometimes taking a stand is scary and uncomfortable, but also necessary and rewarding.

Marcus cleaned up as best he could for Pastor Elliott's visit, noting that he had been eager to talk with him, even to pray with him. Elliott was always concerned about each person's spiritual life, and he was always patient and kind.

He is like nobody I have ever met before, Marcus noted with a smile. *Maybe if I had someone like him in my early years, I wouldn't have ended up here.* He shrugged his shoulders.

Marcus realized that he was in the process of learning more about himself, and Pastor Elliott had everything to do with the positive changes that he was experiencing in the way he thought. Also, he understood that being sent to prison brought on extreme heartache and pain, along with a humility that he had never experienced.

All of his life, he had been taught by words and actions of his father that he was superior to others, especially to women. As painful as it was to face it, Marcus came to see that he had expected his entitlement to follow him through the jury's decision; that his father would somehow get him off from any punishment. *But I deserved punishment for what I did*, he admitted.

While Marcus patiently waited in the visitor center for his session with the pastor, he became lost in his self-evaluation. Marcus slowly began to see the gravity of what he had done.

I killed Dolores, killed her, just because she had disrespected me in front of friends. Who in the world did I think I was?

He cried with remorse while he remembered the many incidents where she had made efforts to get his attention, to please his selfish demands, and put up with his nasty behavior. All she did was with the purpose to persuade him to love her. But there had not been any room in his heart for another person other than himself.

Did I ever love anyone? Maybe Dad?

Marcus knew he would always remember the exact day he had realized that everything he had been taught was a lie. It was a horrible revelation to him when he faced the truth: *I am not... I never was superior to anyone! I was not entitled to have the best in life.* He shook his head in shame as he remembered always looking down at his classmates and friends as if they were inferior.

When did that moment of truth come to him? It was just last week, while he watched his proud father march out of the visitors' center without looking back. As Marcus had watched him, he remembered the words his father had just proclaimed only moments before, and so vehemently.

"You are looking at an honorable man. I have more integrity in my pinkie finger than any other person you may know..."

As Marcus had watched his dad disappear, he saw him in a different light, and then he saw himself in a different light, too. For the first time in his whole life, he felt tremendous remorse for the way he had treated everyone.

Elliott broke Marcus' train of thought as he greeted him at the visitors' booth.

"Hey Marcus, how are you today? Ready for some good conversation and prayer?"

Marcus smiled at his cherished mentor and said, "Oh, yes! I'm looking forward to it!"

They chatted about current happenings within the prison and about events going on with the outside world. Then, Pastor Elliott asked, "Did you get to visit with your father last week?"

Marcus nodded. Elliott continued, "How was your visit? Good?"

"Not good, Pastor, but very productive," Marcus remarked, giving Elliott a thoughtful grin.

Elliott smiled and asked, "Then you did get some details about your mother's mysterious departure and how she can be reached now?"

"No, as we had suspected, any information about my mom will need to come from another source, not from my dad."

Elliott studied his new friend and said, "Please don't allow this temporary setback get you down. The Lord will provide a way."

He gently tapped the glass between them in lieu of affectionately patting Marcus on the shoulder. Elliott waited a few minutes before prodding further.

"Can you talk about your visit? And you mentioned that it had been productive?"

Marcus had known the pastor would be asking for feedback because he had a real interest in what mattered to him. Not because Marcus was special, but because Pastor Elliott was special.

"I came to the realization that my dad has always been a proud, controlling, and arrogant man. Add to that his impatience and quick temper, he has never been easy to get close to. It's even been hard for me because he was never affectionate. I do believe he always loved me, thinking of me as maybe an extension of himself, which would cause me to also be superior to all other people."

Marcus shifted in his seat. "Saying that, I believe he now looks at me much differently. But I look at him—and myself—differently, in a more authentic way. It's sad, but I see it as truly his loss, not mine."

"Wow." Pastor Elliott stared at Marcus for a few moments while he attempted to read the young man's emotions. "Have you experienced a paradigm shift since I last visited you? It seems like it..."

Marcus sheepishly nodded, "Yeah, yeah, I think that's it. I now view everything, or major beliefs that I had been taught, as lacking truth. And I view my father differently, as I guess you could tell by what I just said about him. I see myself as having lived the life of a very spoiled, entitled brat."

He glanced at the pastor, unsure and hesitant whether he should share.

After a pause, he continued, "At night I see dreams, what are really flashbacks of incidents in the past, all examples of his pride and fits of anger, and of mine. I'm thinking, because he was my dad, my only parent, I strived to emulate him. Unfortunately, I have behaved like him in all the bad ways."

He tilted his head. "Not that I'm giving myself excuses. I'm an adult and must accept the things I've thought, said, and did as my responsibility. All of my sins are on me."

Pastor Elliot quickly began to flip through the pages of his Bible.

"Marcus, I can't tell you how glad I am to hear you come to this epiphany. Yes, your sins are on you – but there is a remedy. It's not too late for you!

Let me read to you one of many passages we can find in the Word of God about how pride is something the Lord detests. I'm reading now from Proverbs, Chapter 16, verses 4 through 6, in the Passion Translation."

The Pastor cleared his throat and proceeded to read aloud:

"'The Lord works everything together to accomplish His purpose.
> Even the wicked are included in His plans—
> He sets them aside for the day of disaster.
> Exalting yourself is disgusting to the Lord,
> for pride attracts His punishment—
> and you can count on that!
> You can avoid evil through surrendered worship
> and the fear of God,
> for the power of His faithful love
> removes sin's guilt and grip over you.'"

Marcus wiped a tear from his eye and sniffed while his shoulders crumpled.

"Now that I fully realize how wrong I've been all along, I'm sincerely sorry! I don't want to receive God's punishment, although I know I deserve it; I don't want to live in constant remorse."

Marcus continued to wipe away tears from his eyes and blew his nose into a nearby paper towel.

"I feel tremendous guilt over how I've treated my friends and other people. I even see how I looked at my mother as if she were my servant. Yeah, I was only five, but I was so disrespectful. Did I love her? I don't know. I sure missed her after she left...

"But especially, I can't quit thinking about what I did to Dolores. I don't know what to do with all this guilt, shame, and remorse. Maybe I'll carry it with me from now on." He hung his head. "I'm in the right place. Next stop is Hell."

Elliott gently tapped his fingers on the glass again.

"Son, we've talked about this before. When you are ready, you can take it to the Lord – all of it. He knows your heart. He knows you are sorry for how you were thinking, your treatment of others, and of course, every mean-spirited thing you have done, even taking a life. You can come to Him in repentance, and He will forgive you."

Marcus shook his head, "How is that even possible? Haven't I done the most despicable thing? I am a murderer; I killed her with my bare hands. For what? Because she dissed me?"

Marcus began to sob into his hands.

The pastor explained, "Nobody is perfect, Marcus. Nobody deserves God's mercy. If salvation depended upon how good we are, none would be worthy. That is why Jesus, the only Son of God, had to be sacrificed for our sins. He paid the price for us."

He sympathized with his new friend, watching while Marcus continued to cry. Finally, Marcus pulled himself together to listen further.

"Marcus, do you think that you did anything that the Lord didn't know about, didn't know it was going to happen? Our Creator knows everything! He created the Universe, and yet He knows the number of hairs on your head. He had specific plans for you before you were in your mother's womb!"

Leaning forward, Marcus listened intently.

Pastor Elliot continued, "Ever since the beginning in the Garden of Eden, when Adam and Eve fell into temptations of the Devil, sin has been in the world. There is spiritual warfare going on all around us, good and evil forces in constant battle for our souls. Out of our Heavenly Father's love, He sent His only Son to suffer on the cross, in payment for our sins, and Jesus arose from the grave. He defeated death."

The pastor studied Marcus, who appeared to be absorbing his message.

"To receive what Jesus did for you requires a humble heart of repentance, and a believer's acceptance of Jesus Christ as Lord and Savior," Elliott paused and waited on Marcus to reply.

Marcus questioned with remaining doubts about his ability to be forgiven, "But maybe what I did was so terrible it is unforgivable?"

Pastor Elliott said a silent prayer, *Lord, help me share my wounds to heal his.* He cleared his throat and began sharing his testimony.

"Marcus, you don't know this about me, but I was once a very lost soul. I have made many mistakes; I lived a sinful life, and I took other people down with me when I used drugs and alcohol. I didn't care!"

Tears welled up in his eyes as he continued. "I was the one who introduced my little sister to drugs, and she eventually died of an overdose. She was seventeen, just getting started into an adult life. I think you can imagine the guilt and shame that her death brought."

Their eyes locked in mutual understanding, as if to jointly brace themselves from the dark corners of their lives. The pastor sent up another silent prayer before he continued.

"I'm not proud of my past life of giving in to addictions and supporting my habits, no matter how it harmed other people – my own sister – and myself. But when I came to the Lord, fully repenting and walking away from all that, I knew I was forgiven. I accepted Jesus as my Lord and Savior. My past is now gone, and over time, I finally have forgiven myself. I know I will see my sweet little sister again in Heaven."

He smiled and looked into Marcus' eyes. "I am forever grateful! I am redeemed! This is my ministry: to speak to men like you who have also made terrible mistakes, and to share that God is not finished with you. There *is* a good future for you!"

Marcus looked at the pastor with a renewed hope, timidly saying, "That's what I want, too. I want to be forgiven. But I actually killed..."

His voice trailed off with another surge of doubt, but this time with a glimmer of hope. *Can I be forgiven?*

Encouraging Marcus, Elliott explained, "There are stories of many people in the Bible who had done numerous terrible things, sinned against the Lord, but once they repented, God saw their heart and did forgive them. He can forgive you. You are not forever lost, my friend."

Pastor Elliott showed Marcus his Bible and began, through the glass, to point out scriptures relating to repentance and God's forgiveness. He shared examples of people who had committed horrendous sins and yet, God forgave.

"See here, King David had committed adultery and caused the death of a good man, the woman's husband. Yet when he humbly came to the Lord with a contrite heart, he was forgiven." Pastor Elliott read out loud from 2 Samuel, chapters 11 and 12, which told the story of King David's adultery with Bathsheba, which led him to bring about the death of her husband, Uriah.

Once finished he noted, "Although King David did have conse-quences for these sins — the death of the baby produced in that adulterous relationship — God did forgive him."

Marcus nodded. "I certainly understand the rationale for sin and consequence."

Elliott agreed, "Yes, as do I...Let me give you another example. Saul, the persecutor of Christians, came to face the Lord while on the Damascus road one day, and the Lord blinded him. Saul truly repented and accepted Jesus; he was forgiven. Saul became a new man for the Lord, he was renamed the Apostle Paul, who brought many people to Jesus. Did you know that? He even wrote several books within the New Testament..."

"Yes, I remember this story from my childhood visits to the local Baptist church. I was amazed at the level of mercy he must have received."

The pastor shared with Marcus: salvation was found once a person had genuinely repented and walked away from their sinful living and they believed in Jesus and accepted Jesus Christ as their Lord and Savior.

Pastor Elliott began, "Here, Marcus, is John 3:16, my favorite verse. 'For God so loved the world that He gave His one and only Son, that whoever believes in Him shall not perish but have eternal life.'"[3]

He paused while searching for the next scripture to read, "And we know that Jesus is the way to that salvation when we turn to John 14:6, and Jesus said this Himself, '...I am the way and the truth and the life. No one comes to the Father except through Me.'"⁴

Marcus rallied himself and asked, "Okay. I am ready. What do I need to do?"

The pastor shared that Marcus need only confess with great sincerity, his repentance and acceptance of Jesus Christ. Pastor Elliot shared the salvation message from portions of the Word of God.

"Marcus, here is my version of what is often referred to as the sinner's prayer. Please pray with me."

They both bowed their heads, clasped their hands, and prayed, with Marcus sincerely repeating each phrase after Elliot:

> "Dear Lord, I know I've messed my life up. I ask You to forgive me of all my sins.
>
> Help me with temptations as I strive to walk away from my sinful living.
>
> Dear Jesus, I know you suffered and died on the cross for me,
> to pay for my sins, and You arose from the grave.
> I accept You, Jesus, as my Lord and Savior.
> I ask You to come into my heart now, and
> I will serve You all of my life. In Jesus' name, Amen."⁵

After some minutes had passed, Marcus commented, "You know...I feel different, relieved. It's like a heavy load has been lifted from me." He paused. "I know it sounds crazy because of my circumstance here in prison, but I *am* looking forward to the future now. I have hope."

Pastor Elliott raised his hands upward, "Thank You, Lord, for bringing another man to Your Kingdom! We praise You, Dear God, for Your abounding love, mercy and grace!"

Marcus was beaming with happiness and enthusiastically added, "Amen!"

Before preparing to leave, Pastor Elliott made arrangements for the baptism and instructed Marcus that as he faithfully studied the Word of God, always praying and praising the Lord and (of course) obeying God's commands, he would find himself spiritually growing in his faith.

"Oh, and this is yours, young man, I'll give my Bible to the guard for you before I leave."

"Thank you, Pastor Elliott! I look forward to our next meeting."

Both men were elated. They pretended to bump elbows at the glass that separated them.

The guard, who was also led to Christ by Pastor Elliott, smiled as the pastor handed him his Bible for Marcus, and thought, *Another one added to His Kingdom, praise God!*

Marcus made the most important decision of his life, and it was all about God, His mercy and grace through Jesus Christ. None of us deserve it but salvation can be found when we repent, believe in Jesus, and accept Him. Jesus paid it all, we need only to receive. Have you come to Jesus?

~

Attorney Lewis Sheen, who was also a tax consultant, and Brian met for a working lunch in the cafeteria at Lewis' firm. They discussed financial matters related to Brian's various businesses, looking for the most economically sound and legal methods to follow for future investments and decisions in Brian's portfolio. They were examining potential loopholes.

"Well, that about wraps it," Brian announced, gathering his suit jacket and compiling documents into his briefcase. "As always, I appreciate your assistance."

Lewis looked at his business friend and client of many years. "Hold on for a second." He paused, not sure how he should proceed, since Brian had not mentioned his son during their meeting. "We've been friends for a while now...can you tell me how your son's doing? I mean, he has been incarcerated about a year now, hasn't he?"

Surely, your heart isn't as cold as it seems to be?

Irritated that Lewis would bring this topic up, but also realizing he should share something about Marcus since Lewis had represented him in the trial, Brian sat back down.

"The last visit I had with the boy was several months ago. He accused me of having been abusive to his mother, causing her to abandon him."

Brian's rage at his son's betrayal came rushing forward, and he slammed his fist onto the table. "That was insulting! I felt betrayed. After all, I *raised* that boy by myself!"

He shook his head while his friend listened. "I didn't realize it has been a year already. I do *not* know if I want to see him again, especially if all he wants to do now is grasp at straws into the past. His attempt, I guess, to blame me for his pitiful life."

He shrugged. "It's only his fault...his own doing...that he's rotting in prison..." He paused for a second, realizing how blunt and angry he had sounded. But still, he continued, assuming Lewis would be in agreement.

"I gave him everything I could, did everything for him. I even planned to share with him my business someday, which will soon become an empire. But what did he do? I certainly did *not* raise him to become a murderer."

"Marcus is probably still trying to figure things out. A lot has happened to change his world." Lewis patiently looked at Brian. "Maybe you could simply give him some time to adjust to his new environment. Maybe in time, when you come to see him again, things will be different between the two of you, and you could build from there?"

Irritated with that suggestion, Brian thought, *You're not really offering me any support, buddy.* Then Brian dismissed the topic and stood up, again holding his briefcase.

"Yes, maybe...who knows?" As his way of dismissing the personal conversation, he said, "Well. I will plan to see you next month. My secretary will call to schedule the appointment with you."

"Yes, that's fine," Lewis responded. *Yep. His heart is cold as ice...*

The two men shook hands and Brian left. Lewis watched from his window as his client got into his car and drove off.

What a pompous ass, Lewis thought. *Hmmm. I'll just bet that Marcus had inquired about the whereabouts of his mother. He sure could use someone in his corner right now.*

Remembering Marcus' mother years ago to have been a kind and loving woman, he thought, *I think this is a good time for me to do what I can to help him reunite with his mother...*

Were you surprised at Brian's take on his last visit with Marcus, and at his continued lack of empathy? What might it take to change his mindset?

Marcus was alone in his cell late at night, praying as he always did since he had turned his life over to Jesus. But this night he was burdened with the news he had learned through the prison grapevine. He fervently prayed out loud for Killer, his enemy:

"Dear Heavenly Father,
You are an awesome God, Maker of Heaven and Earth,
of all living things. I praise You and I thank you for all that You have done for me. Thank you for sending Your only Son, Jesus, to pay for my sins; and He arose! Lord, today I heard that my past cellmate who had kept me in fear, Killer, is now in the infirmary at another prison, possibly near death's door. I understand that he has committed crimes, and probably incited the assault
he suffered by other inmates, but my heart goes out to him.

As You know, Lord, I forgave him of the tormenting threats he piled upon me while we shared our cell, and I now pray for his soul.
If he could only understand the truth in the spiritual law that
we will reap what we sow, if only he knew that Heaven and Hell are real, and if only he repented and accepted Jesus, he would not be a lost soul. I ask you then, Father, forgive him, for he knows not what he does!

Bring him conviction for his evil past; bring him people who will lead him to salvation in Jesus. And please bring him healing and a future in his Christian walk. Lord, show him how to put on the full armor of God as described in Ephesians, so he will be equipped in the days to come while the enemy attacks.

Even, Lord, I ask you to show him what his unique calling in life is. And with that Lord, I know You created me for a purpose to be fulfilled. I ask You to show me what my calling in life is, and I ask for the Holy Spirit to guide me in it. In Jesus' precious name, Amen."

Early the next morning, a guard announced, "Marcus, you have a visitor this morning, the pastor. Get ready."

Wow! Marcus thought, *This is perfect timing, God's timing!*

After the two men greeted each other, the pastor asked, "Marcus, I woke up with you on my mind early this morning, and I felt I should come see you. Can you share with me what's going on with you?"

"I need your help!" Marcus blurted out.

Intrigued, Elliot nodded for him to continue.

"I know Killer, my past cellmate that I have talked with you about, is in a prison infirmary, near death." He touched the glass that separated them with an expression of urgency. "He doesn't know Jesus! I have prayed for him. You have access, and so I ask you to quickly go see him and bring him to the Lord."

Pastor Elliot was elated with the obvious change in Marcus. Not only was Marcus able to forgive Killer for causing him months of fear, but also he now has genuine concern for that man's soul. Elliot immediately agreed.

"Well my friend, I see this is why I felt compelled to see you. I can get specific details from the prison administration about this man and where I can find him. And I will be on my way now to do this very thing."

They prayed together and the pastor quickly went out to pursue this special mission.

Marcus smiled and breathed a short prayer, "Thank you Lord for bringing Elliot along to do what I'm unable to do, all to Your glory..."

Do you have enemies that need to be forgiven? We forgive for our soul's sake. How many times must we forgive? Jesus told Peter seventy times seven in Matthew 18:21-22. That means repeatedly!

Can you go further, and even pray for your enemy's soul? This is what Jesus tells us to do, in Matthew 5:43-48.

It appears Marcus has come full circle!

~

On the two-year mark of Marcus' incarceration, he awoke in the morning with excitement, knowing he would see Pastor Elliott that afternoon. Since his decision to accept Jesus, he daily read and studied the Word of God and prayed.

Now, I think I can understand how the Apostle Paul felt content, regardless of where he might be or the station of life he was in at the moment.

Like himself, the Apostle Paul had spent much of his time in prison. Over time, Marcus learned to be thankful for what he had, and to praise the Lord, even in his circumstance. He felt that he did indeed learn to be content, regardless of his environment.

This life, here in prison and on earth is temporary. I can focus on Jesus... and on eternity in His Kingdom!

During the night, he had dreamed...or was it a vision? That, like the Apostle Paul, he, too, was called to minister to men in prison. He felt as if his heart would explode with an urgency, feeling that now was the appropriate time for him to begin his ministry.

"My ministry!" Marcus whispered into the air. "Thank you, Jesus! What the enemy meant for my harm, You have made it for good."

He was eager to share this great news with his mentor, friend, and pastor. Marcus knew full well that Pastor Elliott would be overjoyed with this enormous decision along his Christian walk, and the pastor would certainly offer his assistance in this calling.

But Marcus was in for a surprise himself.

With a number of failed attempts and many hours of time (because Marcus' mother had changed her name a few times, and her address several times), it had taken Attorney Sheen nearly a year to find the boy's mother. Once found, it took much persuasion to convince her that it was not too late to reunite with her son. Attorney Sheen shared this information with Pastor Elliott, who agreed to be the conduit between mother and son.

Pastor Elliott was elated to find that Marcus' mother was a fine Christian woman who did work in outreaches for the poor. But Elliott still had some work to do. She was terribly fearful that Marcus would judge her harshly and reject her. She also believed that to see her again after all these years may rekindle Marcus' hurt and anger over her abandonment. Especially, she feared Brian may get wind of their reunion and would make good on all the horrible threats of violence he had promised.

Elliott patiently worked with her about these fears. Finally, agreeing fear and faith had no place together, she must choose one.

What brought her to rally the courage to face her fears was the knowledge that Marcus had accepted Jesus as his Lord and Savior. Finally, the two had agreed that Elliott was to first talk with Marcus about the idea of them meeting again, although Elliott felt confident that he knew his friend's heart.

Were you excited for Marcus to have discovered his calling? Do you know what your unique purpose in life is? When you pray about it, the Lord will answer.

Have you ever been so afraid that your fear kept you from experiencing something great? The enemy uses fear to battle against our faith. We cannot have both fear and faith – we must choose one or the other!

$\approx$

"Today's the day!" Marcus shouted. He was overcome with excitement.

After six months of conversations back and forth through Pastor Elliott, he would see the answer to his prayers: that she would be alive, he would get to visit with his mother, and especially, he would be able to develop a relationship with her. He fully understood her hesitation, but she had nothing to be fearful about.

He told himself, *Dad has essentially stopped visiting me. And that is absolutely okay. I will continue to pray for my father, for his salvation.*

But I do not need to see him as he is right now...haughty, mean-spirited, and toxic.

I learned about domestic violence in my quest to understand what happened in my family. I was in a toxic environment with my mother and father as a child. As a young adult, I was abusive too. I can only imagine what my mother must have experienced. I know that to pursue peace sometimes requires a person to safely leave that dangerous and habitually toxic environment.

*I wish Mom had known she could have contacted **The National Domestic Violence Hotline number, 1-800-799-7233 (SAFE).** She could have received expert advice on devising an escape plan, and maybe I could have gone with her.*[6]

But then, her situation happened years ago; maybe there were no resources back then? Regardless, I know my mother felt she had no choice but to leave; her life was at stake.

Marcus sat at the booth in the visitors' center, too excited and nervous to remain calm. Like a dream, he saw his mother come through the door with what he imagined to be the aura of lights all around her. He recognized her immediately.

She is beautiful! he gasped.

They smiled at each other as she sat in the chair facing him. They each instinctively placed their hands on the glass between them.

They cried. Moments later, they thought to pick up their phone receivers.

Sincerely and without hesitation, Marcus blurted out, "Mom, I love you!"

THINGS TO PONDER

What a blessing to experience answered prayers! Have you received answers to your prayers? Maybe it didn't look like what you had expected, you are still waiting, or the answer may be no. I encourage you to have patient faith in the Lord.

Remember this: whatever harm or evil the enemy may intend for you, God always has a good plan for your life. A great example is the story of Joseph and his brothers in Genesis, chapters 37 through 50.

*For reference material regarding domestic violence, go to
https://CarinJayneCasey.com.*

Before leaving this story, could you take a few moments to think about each character? What decisions did they make in response to good or evil, and what were their rewards or consequences? Could you see the potential influences surrounding them in making each decision? How and when did they put on their armor of God?

I ask you to consider, who is directing your steps?

TWO

WHICH PATH WILL YOU TAKE?
GOING BEYOND A GREEDY, ENVIOUS ATTITUDE

Two women from differing walks in life are travelers who happen to meet on a train to Chicago. One is running away from something while the other is in pursuit of a conquest. Will they find a common interest for collaboration? Will they learn valuable lessons from each other?

"How many tickets?" said the booking clerk at the ticket booking window of the Lawrence, Kansas AMTRAK railway station. [1]

He looked into the eyes of a stressed young woman before him and believed she might be confused, asking, "Lady, are you okay?"

Becky forced herself to concentrate on what the booking clerk was saying while her mind raced. *Oh...where am I going? It needs to be a big city, far enough away from here...*

She composed herself. "Good morning, sir, I'd like one ticket to Chicago please, the earliest available."

While the booking clerk gazed at his documentation for that location and available times, he also glanced at the huge luggage bags she had with her, "Is that round trip or one-way?"

Becky quickly responded, "One way."

"Yes, that will be train number 7501, at 9:05 pm, $32.00 for one way to Chicago today. Boarding will begin in 20 minutes. You're in luck, we've not yet implemented the additional charge for overweight bags, but it may be enforced by the time you decide to return."

She nodded agreement and began rummaging through her large purse. While he waited for her to produce money or a credit card, he inquired, "Will you be needing help with your luggage? We can have someone carry it out for you now, $5.00."

"Yes, please," she responded while counting the money out from a large wad of bills.

He made change for a fifty, and she quickly crammed the remainder back into her purse and looked around to see if anyone had been watching.

"Lady, I must read to you all of the latest restrictions as a result of the worldwide COVID-19 virus."

With gloved hands, he handed her a copy to read along while he read the regulations to her; the page was encased in plastic. After he had completed reading, Becky responded, "I understand."

Almost simultaneously, the booking clerk handed her the ticket and snapped his fingers, motioning for a nearby porter.

"Oh, you do realize, this train runs through the night and we do not guarantee arrival earlier than 7:00 am, right?"

She nodded agreement.

A porter suddenly appeared with a luggage rack, grabbed the bags, and looked at the booking clerk, who quickly shouted, "7501 to Chicago, 9:05..."

The porter nodded, received the five dollars from Becky, and disappeared with the luggage.

Nervously, Becky watched her luggage being hauled away. Her eyes searched the boarding area for the least noticeable bench area and rushed over to it; she positioned herself on a bench. She closed her eyes and attempted to relax with deep breathing exercises.

They deserved it anyway, for being such losers, and for causing my child-hood to be a life of lack.

She felt pangs of guilt again, knowing her parents and her church family had trusted her.

Ignoring feelings of remorse, Becky decided to look instead at her success, and that she is now safe from being caught. She closed her eyes to take a nap.

I deserve a good rest! She thought, *After a year of cultivating confidences of people I eventually had intentions to bilk, and then more than two months of hard labor into the specifics of this scam to get myself to this point...*

Well, what have we here? Is Becky an amateur con-artist who struggles with her conscience? Having free will, the choice is hers to make. Let us hope that the light in her wins over the darkness, as in John 1:5 in the New Living Translation (NLT):

The light shines in the darkness, and the darkness can never extinguish it.

Unknown to Becky and from another life entirely was precious, haughty little Emily. She was raised in a prosperous family as the only child and expected to continue the life of a princess throughout her adulthood.

She scanned a woman in the opposite car who did not have designer clothes and held a purse that was an obvious knock-off.

Oh, brother, how did she manage to get into this business class section? She does not know her place! Maybe I should complain?

She laughed at the embarrassment she could cause.

Emily believed that she should have advantages over others and remained envious of those who seemed to have more wealth and prestige than she did. On occasion, Emily liked to think of herself as moral and religious, but she was aware of the darkness that lurked in her heart. Her parents worshipped her, and boyfriends lavished their time, gifts, and services on her.

The whole world thinks highly of me, as it should! Emily told herself confidently.

Emily enjoyed her favorite YouTube channel on her laptop in her special business class section of the train, excited to begin her adventures in the Windy City. While people at this brief stop bustled about boarding, she allowed herself to people-watch.

How quaint, she thought as she assessed the value of their luggage and attire. Suddenly Emily laughed out loud.

Oh, look at that! Even a hobo would know that plaid and stripes do not match!

With the sound of her laughter, the old man wearing his favorite striped shirt stopped to smile at her. Leaning with one hand on his cane, he was able to tip his plaid hat to this beautiful young woman.

Ahh, he recalled, *my Rachel was just as lovely before she passed.*

After all of the passengers had settled, the train continued the route to Chicago.

While Emily appears spoiled from the best in life, Becky came from a life of lack. Will they meet? Collaborate their scam-games? It will be interesting to see what influence, if any, they will have on each other...

Becky decided to check out the people on the train, thinking, *Hum, you never know where another good start may be...*

Just as Becky began to pass a very well-dressed woman in the lounge car, that woman suddenly grabbed her attention by greeting, "Hi, how are you today? Would you like to sit at my table?"

She motioned for Becky to sit opposite her. Becky thought, *Geez, I guess...maybe this is opportunity knocking?*

Becky considered this encounter as potential for a venture and responded, "Well, not at *your* table, but how about here, across the aisle? We can still hear each other..."

The woman nodded agreement, and Becky continued, "I presume you're headed for Chicago?"

"Yes, I'm returning after a luxuriant spa retreat." She smiled, "My name is Emily."

Emily held out her hand that displayed a diamond tennis bracelet and an exquisite ring of a pear-shaped emerald encased with diamonds.

Yes, my dear, admire my jewelry pieces. Don't you wish you had them too? ha ha.

Becky was indeed impressed, but she knew she should not let it show. She shifted her gaze from the diamond display and looked into this beautiful and obviously rich woman's big brown eyes.

"Glad to meet you! I'm Becky...this is my first time into Chicago. Thought I'd check it out, and if I like it, who knows? Maybe I'll stay a while."

They fell into chit chat about the food available for snacks, and they discussed the anticipated weather in Chicago.

Becky wondered and asked herself, *Sure, I talk the talk to myself, but am I really willing and able to encourage this fine woman to share some of the excessive wealth she so proudly exhibits? Am I sure this is the path I want to take?*

"Tell me, Becky, do you have a place to stay and plans for employment?" Emily casually asked, full of self-confidence in her ability to win Becky over with her smooth sales pitch, especially after observing that Becky appeared intrigued with her bait-baubles.

Look to me, you poor little country girl, and maybe you will learn a thing or two!

Becky hadn't anticipated a stranger to ask about her job status, and so quickly into the conversation. *Hum,* she wondered, *is she already scouting or checking me out?*

"I have submitted a few job applications," Becky calmly answered while dabbing a napkin at her mouth. "While in wait for their response, I thought I'd start by treating myself to a mini-vacation at a casual bed and breakfast, Villa D' Citta...maybe you've heard of it?"

"Oh, yes," Emily enthusiastically responded, "that location is perfect for shopping." She added, "I dine in the Lincoln Park district often. Maybe we could meet for dinner this evening?"

Where I can run my fabulous sales pitch on you...

She looked into Becky's eyes to search for intrigue, thinking, *Oh my! It is so much easier when I am working my charms on a man...*

She allowed herself to pause only a few moments, adding, "After all, I live in Chicago..."

Becky affirmed her suspicions to herself, thinking, *This Miss Emily is already preparing me for her sales pitch! I think I had better tread carefully...*

Emily changed posture, leaning in for emphasis. "And, when I was your age, I sure *did* appreciate the wisdom of experienced, successful women in the business world." She paused, attempting to read the effect she had on Becky.

Nope, I have not hooked her yet...

"Besides, I know *all* of the best shops to go to, of course, for quality, name-brand items." She gazed with secret disapproval at Becky's mediocre attire and cheap jewelry.

Good grief, girl, you should be hungry for a financial opportunity!

Becky carefully agreed, saying, "I'd love that."

At the same instant she cautioned herself, *This woman is extremely confident! She might be planning to take me for a terrible ride! Becky, beware! After all, Chicago is her playground!*

The two women continued in fun, carefree conversation. As they talked, Becky gathered information.

Emily has apparently always been the spoiled, only child, grown to expect and get whatever from family and boyfriends. And yet, Becky thought, smiling while Emily seemed to be going into the introduction to a sales pitch, *she appears to work hard at selling and getting, always wanting more. Isn't that just a bit sad?*

Another woman who apparently knew Emily walked over while adjusting her royal blue satin face mask and positioned herself with one arm leaning on the seat-frame in front of Emily.

"Oh, look at you Emily darling, I never expected to find you on this train today. And who is your friend you're talking with?"

Becky quickly sized up the older woman as of a higher prestige and more wealth than Emily.

Wow, this is a whole different class than I am accustomed to. Quickly losing confidence in herself, she thought, *I had better be brushing up on appropriate protocol or get out of the pool!*

Emily smiled and gave introductions. "Ms. Turner, this is Becky, whom I just met."

Please do not assume she is my friend!

Once the two smiled at each other, Emily motioned with her hand, saying, "And Becky...Ms. Turner, a dear, long-time friend of my family."

Becky smiled. "I'm pleased to meet you, Ms. Turner."

As her gaze lingered on the older woman's Serpenti brooch, she thought, *Man, that must be 18 karat white gold, and with pave diamonds, I would imagine worth twenty-thousand dollars! Wearing that on a train! Is she nuts?*

Ms. Turner and Emily went down memory lane for Becky's benefit, sharing about their many travels within the United States and abroad. Becky found it fascinating since she had not been out of state before, much less out of the country.

Becky thought, *Ms. Turner is such a nice woman, and interesting. I love to listen to her talk about her travels...it's like I can imagine myself being there!*

After small talk for a few more minutes, they all said their farewells and Ms. Turner straightened up. She carefully moved along toward another car.

As Ms. Turner walked out of sight and while Emily was still smiling, she commented, "That ol' cow has *so* much more than she deserves."

"What?" Becky asked, sincerely confused.

Your words sound so much like my own thoughts I might have had recently. But look at yourself, you little Richie-Bitchie!

Noticing the surprise in Becky, Emily felt she should elaborate, "It's just that, she was born into wealth and always has been given whatever she wants. She throws away more than I may ever have!" Realizing she had overshared, but feeling justified, she continued saying, "Well, sometimes life just isn't fair, is it?"

Becky lamely gave a response. "Yeah, I guess I know what you mean..."

Not really...Emily, can you see yourself? Didn't you just describe your own life?

While their conversation continued, Becky remained bewildered, trying to understand what she had just witnessed. *Emily, an obvious rich gal herself...born and raised in it from her own story...said things I might have said...thoughts that I have had!*

What? Is there no end to it? Will I be like Emily once I reach that golden pie, and remain bitter, jealous, and never satisfied? Is that the punishment we live with for what we do? Are we doomed because of our unquenchable desires for money, wealth, and prestige?

Emily tried to get Becky to commit to meeting for dinner at a specific time and place, but Becky's mind seemed to be elsewhere.

Well, if it happens, it happens Emily told herself, *at least I have her phone number.* She looked at Becky, thinking, *Okay, I will let you have a break for now, but watch out if you come for dinner tonight, because I am well able to manipulate you.*

The two women parted company and returned to their own respective cars.

This goes to demonstrate that the evil poison of envy can attack any of us, regardless of our station in life. The enemy tempts us with it in hopes to steal our peace. We find encouragement from Jesus in the following passage:

A thief has only one thing in mind—he wants to steal, slaughter, and destroy. But I have come to give you everything in abundance, more than you expect—life in its fullness until you overflow!

John 10:10, The Passion Translation (TPT)

Emily ordered a mixed drink to soothe her soul but could not resist allowing herself to revisit the short, but disturbing encounter with Ms. Turner. As she compared herself to Ms. Turner, she smoldered with anger and jealousy, causing the onslaught of a painful stress headache.

Yes, you old bag, I noticed that expensive brooch.

Visualizing the brooch brought on more excruciating headache pain, but she continued to concentrate on it. *Worth more than any piece of jewelry I have!*

She added a past hurt to her reasons for envy. *Ms. Turner got to explore Europe, going to all the places I should have gone to!*

Emily seethed, *Oh, no, Dad refused to pay for my trip to Germany and Italy, even after I begged, and so did dumb-ass Joe.*

She consoled herself, thinking, *Yeah, I bet Joe wishes he had paid it now that I've dumped him. He will never find a woman as good as me.* She took another sip of her drink and closed her eyes, hoping to relax. *But I will get there — without any of them! I need no one but myself. I am self-sufficient and successful on my own!*

We are warned about a prideful and envious attitude in James 3:14-16, in The Passion Translation (TPT):

But if there is bitter jealousy or competition hiding in your heart, then don't deny it and try to compensate for it by boasting and being phony. For that has nothing to do with God's heavenly wisdom but can best be described as the wisdom of this world, both selfish and devilish. So wherever jealous and selfishness are uncovered, you will also find many troubles and every kind of meanness.

Becky sat in her seat, unable to get over the scene she had just experienced. She came to realize the sad truth of her life through Emily's plight.

I look at Emily as someone to envy. I want, I deserve to have what she has. And I vow to find a way to get it. Even if it means to take from others, to take from her! But it looks like Emily and I are both on a familiar path, only she's ahead of me...And yet, we seem to remain in the same spot.

Becky fully realized that this is where the confusion... no, where the truth is.

Okay, regardless of our environments, she seems to have exactly the same attitude that I have. How can that be? I watch her, full of envy over what Ms. Turner has. She feels she deserves so much more.

Sadly, Becky's assessment brought her to face the bottom line: *I don't see any satisfaction in this life to come for Emily...or for me...with this need for material wealth, this never-ending need for monetary gain...*

She finally admitted to herself, *With this greedy mindset, I will never find satisfaction or peace in my life.*

Becky's thoughts went back to the church congregation and to the community, to the folks she had just scammed.

Haven't I heard preachin' about this very thing? What lies in a man's heart, so is he? If my heart is full of greed and envy, what...who am I? What kind of future can I hope for...unless I change?

Becky rubbed her forehead; the mental conflict was painful. Quickly, she found aspirin in her purse and downed them with a glass of ice water.

I cannot think about this right now. I'm not ready to make any decisions. Maybe later...need to be calm and rest.

Becky fell asleep.

Have you ever been in conflicting turmoil (in a battle between good and evil), only to put off significant decision-making? I have learned (the hard way) that when I did not make a positive decision, that inaction was a decision I had to live with. Results can be disastrous!

Don't put it off; do it now! Don't rest until you do.

Save yourself like a gazelle escaping from a hunter, like a bird fleeing from a net.

Proverbs 6:4-16, New Living Translation (NLT)

Around three o'clock in the morning, Becky began to have horrible nightmares.

She watched her parents cry because they could not provide their precious daughter with proper shoes and clothing for her first day of school. Their hearts broke every time they had to tell her that she could not join the Girl Scouts, become a cheerleader, or play an instrument in the band.

Oddly, in her dream Becky could hear part of her parent's conversation.

Her father looked like a broken man, saying, "We spent all we could every year for her birthday and Christmas, all we could!"

Becky's mother responded, "Honey, you know it was not enough to make her happy." Her voice trailed off with the echoing words, "not enough...not enough."

They embraced in sorrow, sobbing.

Becky felt their heartbreak as if it were her own. She watched them experience great despair and pain during her teenage years, while she screamed words of hatred toward them because they were poor. Within this dream, Becky realized, *Oh, God, they knew I was ashamed of them.*

Becky woke up drenched in sweat, tears, and regret.

"What have I done?" she shouted into the air, not realizing for a moment that she was still on the train; she cried bitterly.

She literally heard evil whispers from the enemy and then mumbled the same words to herself over and over:

"Becky, you are lost, there is no turning back for you. There is nothing you can do now. Lost..."

I have a confession. Long ago I was on the brink of deciding to let go of something I knew was sinful, but I decided to sleep on it and make that decision in the morning. All night long, the Lord gave me dreams that were so real, it could have been videos I watched. It brought me over-whelming conviction and during the early morning hours I repented. Knowing my heart, the Lord forgave me. I am thankful for His 'videos' and since then I have prayed for others who were astray, "Lord, please show them Your path; give them Your 'videos'!"

In our spiritual battle, while the Lord brings conviction to us for our soul's sake, the Devil also comes along to turn that conviction into condemnation, so you will feel hopeless and forever lost. Those are lies of the enemy! In the following scripture, Jesus announces the enemy as a liar:

...He was a murderer from the beginning.
He has always hated the truth, because there is no truth in him.
When he lies, it is consistent with his character; for he is a liar and the father of lies.
John 8:43-44, New Living Translation (NLT)

Once the train had stopped at 7:10 am and passengers were allowed to get their things and exit in a slow, orderly manner within social distancing requirements, Emily quickly looked for Becky, fully intending to make a solid effort to get her commitment for dinner.

Who knows? Emily thought. *She may very well become a fruitful venture for me.* Smiling with confidence at her expertise in sales pitch, she surmised, *And likely very quick and easy, at that!*

But when she did see Becky, she saw a sad mess with darkened eyes. "What happened to you?" she blurted out.

She realized how insensitive that sounded, so she followed up with her hand giving a light touch to Becky's shoulder, with a voice that oozed with fake concern and asked, "Are you okay? Is there anything I can do to help?"

Becky gave this new acquaintance a small smile (having decided during the night *not* to become friends with her) and said, "Oh, I'm okay, just didn't sleep well." She rallied herself, adding, "I'll be fine once I'm settled in my room…"

Becky wanted to tell her, *Get out of my space! Stop touching me! Didn't you see last night I do not want you in my space, you Richie-Bitchie?*

Emily reminded Becky, "Oh, yes, once you're rested, we can have dinner and plan our shopping spree!"

She looked at Becky's sluggish demeanor and decided to work her pitch once they had met at a restaurant, not feeling as confident that she would have that opportunity.

"Okay, I have your number, and here is my business card. Call me!" She grabbed her luggage, and as she walked on, adding, "Since you seem to be under the weather, dinner will be my treat!"

Emily fussed at herself as she continued along her way, thinking, *Stop the begging! You always do better when you select a man to charm, anyway!*

Becky waved cheerily. "Thank you, have a nice day!"

While she stood and watched Emily disappear into the crowd of people, she whispered under her breath with great resolve, "Nope.

That's one thing I am sure of: I am not planning to meet with you, Emily, darling..."

Have you ever had to stop from going further in a relationship because you sensed danger ahead? It is often awkward or painful to walk away; but heeding to those warnings is so important! You may call it instinct or listening to your gut, but I believe it is the Holy Spirit's promptings. Let us look at John 14:26, in the New Living Translation (NLT) (emphasis added):

But when the Father sends the Advocate as my representative—that is, the Holy Spirit—He will teach you everything and will remind you of everything I have told you.

Becky's room at the Villa D' Citta was much nicer than she had imagined. After unpacking her luggage and finding a good hiding place for the stash, she froze with the money in her hand and stared at each bill in front of her.

She mumbled, "The love of money..." She paused, struggling to remember the rest of that phrase she remembered reading in the Bible. "The love of money is the root of all evil."

She shook her head, quickly put the money away, and fussed at herself, "Stop thinking so much!" She glanced at her clothing. "I'll feel better after a good shower and breakfast at the Café, and no more thinking until then!"

After her shower, she grabbed a notepad to take notes, and rushed to the cafe, realizing how hungry she had become. While scanning the breakfast menu and sipping on her coffee, she allowed herself to revisit the sad quandary she was in.

Suddenly, her thoughts were interrupted by a couple standing close to her table. She looked up and shook with fright, thinking, *What? Pastor Henderson and his wife? Oh my God!*

"Hello, Becky," Pastor Henderson said softly while smiling kindly at her. "How was your trip to Chicago?"

His wife added, "We drove up, just arriving here ourselves."

They waited to be invited to sit at the table. Without receiving an immediate invitation, the pastor asked, "May we sit with you, dear? We tested negative for the virus, and have had our vaccinations..."

Becky gulped down her fears, thinking, *Maybe, I hope, this is just a terrible coincidence?*

With forced positive energy, she responded, "Oh, yes, please sit down. It is so nice to see the both of you. What brings you here?"

After silently pulling out a chair for his wife, the pastor sat down at Becky's table. They removed their face masks and looked directly into Becky's eyes.

"We came for you, of course," the pastor responded. Firmly pointing his finger onto the table, he continued, "You are *not* the first person to get cold feet and run on us..."

Startled, Becky gasped. *I have been caught!*

Seeing the fear in Becky's eyes, the pastor's wife quickly explained, "We came to offer an olive branch, Becky, not to pass judgement or to cause you grief."

Becky began to cry, mumbling, "I'm so sorry. I'm so very... sorry..."

While she cried, her remorse grew. Breaking social distancing protocol, the Hendersons hugged her and held her while she cried.

After a few minutes had passed, the pastor handed Becky a handkerchief. "Here. Pull yourself together, honey. We need to talk."

Becky dabbed at her eyes with the handkerchief, asking, "How did you find me? And how did you know so quickly that I had taken off?"

The pastor's wife patted Becky's hand. "Oh, we had an idea that you were going to do this from the start, so we had someone watching you." She paused, then added, "And then you didn't contact the folks at the mission once you had the money accumulated...that was a resounding red flag."

Becky looked into their sweet and honest eyes with amazement. "And you just let me run? Let it happen?"

"Becky. You don't realize what we already know about you," said Pastor Henderson.

Becky held her breath, not sure she wanted to hear what he had to say next. *What is it they already know about me?*

As if he had heard her thoughts, he said, "We know that, regardless of your current choices, you are stepping into the path of what God created you for. You are on the cusp of your calling." Pastor Henderson concluded, "The Lord has shared this with us. Today, you are the one sheep who has gone astray, only temporarily, and we're here to bring you back into the fold."

"What?" Becky could hardly believe this. "To bring me back? Isn't it too late for that?"

The pastor's wife reassured her, saying, "Becky, we were with you when you accepted Jesus as your Lord and Savior; we were with you when you insisted on being baptized, even at only twelve years old. We absolutely know your heart."

"Look what I have done! How can you see any good in me?"

Pastor Henderson explained, "We know it was not an easy life for you, especially once you became a teenager, trying to fit in with friends who were much better off than yourself. And in that, the enemy tempted you, and told you lies."

His wife confirmed her husband's statement and added, "Yes, and for a short while you've been ...well, distracted." She paused for effect. "But I believe you now see the err of your ways."

Pastor Henderson interjected, "You have a great future in store, serving the Lord!"

"Then, you're not angry with me? And despite what I've done, you believe in my future?"

They shook their heads, and the pastor continued, "No, no anger! But we would like to pray with you. If you are ready, we would like to encourage and assist you... as you approach the Lord in repentance. Are you ready for that now? Do you need time to think about it?"

Eager to get her past behavior behind her and to have a clean slate with the Lord, Becky responded, "Oh, yes, I spent the entire night believing there was no hope for me. I kept hearing and telling myself that I was lost forever! I want to ask for God's forgiveness now." She looked into their eyes and added, "And for your forgiveness."

Pastor Henderson solemnly stated, "Please bow your head, and pray this with me out loud."

They all bowed their heads; the pastor's wife and Becky repeated each phrase after him.

"Dear Heavenly Father, I have sinned against you and against people who trusted me. I humbly come to you now with a contrite heart, asking for your forgiveness. I repent of my sins, all of them, and I promise to pay full restitution for what I have taken. Please strongly guide me to make good decisions in the future. Thank you, dear Lord, for loving me, In Jesus' name, Amen."

After the prayer, Becky felt as if a huge weight had been lifted from her. She cried again, but this time with relief and happiness.

Thank you, Lord! For your love and mercy! Becky fully knew how very close she had been to reaching the side of destruction, her heart swelled with relief. *I am sincerely grateful, and I will serve You all the days of my life!*

The pastor's wife clarified, "And dear, you do have our forgiveness."

They were all filled with peace and joy.

Pastor Henderson then revealed something that would significantly impact Becky, "The truth is, we didn't tell anyone what we knew was happening. As far as everyone else knows to this point, you are *in the process* of giving the mission folks what you had accumulated in your fundraiser from the church family and from the community. And, other than this short detour, that is still the plan. Am I correct?"

Becky was elated at what she thought she had just heard but asked for clarification. "Pastor, do you mean I can actually do what I had started to do in this fundraiser, and nobody needs to know about my terrible...detour?"

"That is correct, Becky, dear," answered the pastor's wife. "The enemy worked hard to sway your intentions toward harming others, but he has failed. Now you can see clearly; you can walk into your calling. It is your choice."

"Yes...yes! That *is* what I want to do!" She openly hugged the couple and almost kissed them, but suddenly remembered social distancing protocol, and stopped herself. "I want you both to come to my room now and I'll give you the money to be sent today to the mission. I can't wait to get it out of my possession!" She paused. "It's all there. I've only spent my own money to this point, money that had already been saved up for emergencies."

Pastor Henderson instructed, "This is still *your* project, not ours. We will all go together to get the funds wired to the appropriate mission staff after our breakfast together. Then, my wife and I will be heading home, and you can spend another few days for a period of refresh, alone with the Lord." He paused, looking to his wife for agreement before saying, "That is our treat."

Becky thought to herself, *Wow, they trust me this much, even after what I've done? Their forgiveness is real.*

How easy it could have been for the Hendersons to have brought Becky's mistake to the attention of the authorities instead of giving her the opportunity to repent and continue in the path that the Lord had laid out for her. In their actions, they were taking on the character of Jesus, that of loving forgiveness. They had faith that the Lord had a good plan for Becky's life.

Above all, have fervent and unfailing love for one another,
because love covers a multitude of sins
[it overlooks unkindness and unselfishly seeks the best for others].
1 Peter 4:8, Amplified Bible (AMP)

After the funds were safely headed for the mission as originally intended, Becky and the Hendersons prayed together and then parted company.

After they had left, Becky decided to enjoy the rest of the day shopping and dining, full of gratitude to the Lord and to the Hendersons for giving her this opportunity for positive change.

While she shopped, she found items that her parents would like.

All I want to do now is to go home, tell Mom and Dad how much I love them, and to apologize for the several times I have been disrespectful. I was downright mean to them.

She received several calls on her cell phone, and she recognized them as being from Emily. But Becky's resolve remained. *No, I feel like the Lord is warning me not to respond. I think my turn back to the Lord does not include a relationship with her. But I wish her well, and my prayers go out to her.*

After an early and delicious dinner at the Alinea, Becky walked out with her next destination in mind: the AMTRAK railway station. As she glanced back at the restaurant, she thought she saw Emily waltzing into the restaurant from another direction.

Becky considered calling out to greet her as a kind gesture, but swiftly something inside her warned, *No, let her go. She is not part of your destiny.*

After spending the past five years ignoring the still small voice of the Lord, Becky was determined to make up for the wasted time spent in greed, anger, pride, and envy.

Now, because of my rededication to the Lord, my entire outlook has changed... I am back on track for an overflowing life of abundance – of inner joy and peace!

Becky smiled, thinking, *Thank You for Your mercy, for the grace; thank You for the blood of Jesus Christ!*

Praise the Lord that He is a merciful and loving God! Let us look at Hebrews 13:5 in the English Standard Version (ESV) (emphasis added), which appears to briefly address where Becky had been headed, and where her heart now lies:

Keep your life free from love of money, and be content with what you have, for He has said, "I will never leave you nor forsake you."

Although Emily had called Becky's cell number several times and left messages at the Villa, Emily was unable to reach Becky.

Well, it appears that simple country gal has escaped me.

With the day already pushing noon, Emily decided to move on to another plan in search of prospects.

Next! No wasting time for me. She perused the traveler's guide for high-end restaurants near the Lincoln District, since she had positioned herself in that area to pursue Becky.

Ah, this looks good. Alinea, American fare. She called and made reservations for two. *I think I will play the jilted woman scene again. But for now, I must rest well. I must be at my best appearance for tonight's performance...*

Hours later, Emily awoke, showered, and meticulously applied make-up. She arranged her hair and selected a well-fitting, somewhat sexy dress.

She looked at herself in the mirror. *All dressed up for meeting my gallant hero...*

Have you ever encountered someone who always had a scheme? How does the Lord view this life choice? Let us look at what the Word of God says:

*There are six things that the Lord **hates**, seven that are an abomination to Him:*
haughty eyes, a lying tongue, and hands that shed innocent blood,
a heart that devises wicked plans, feet that make haste to run to evil,
a false witness who breathes out lies, and one who sows discord among brothers.
Proverbs 6:16-19, English Standard Version (ESV) (emphasis added)

As planned, Emily sat at her table, anxiously looking at the door occasionally while she nursed her wine. She could tell that she had already snagged the attention of a handsome and wealthy looking man in the corner, who appeared to be by himself.

Purrr-fect!

Once certain this man was watching, Emily pulled her cell phone out, gazed at it, texted, then looked again, ending with the appearance she had received disappointing news.

I am such a great actress, she told herself.

The waiter came to her table, offering to bring an appetizer while she continued to wait. Looking slightly distressed, she said she would go ahead and order; she would be eating alone after all. With that, the waiter removed the extra menu and glass.

With this cue, that wealthy-looking man quickly placed his face mask back on and waltzed over to her table and greeted her with a friendly smile.

"Hello, my lady, I just happened to notice that you're apparently dining alone, as I am. Would you like some company?"

Wow, you are even more beautiful up close!

He explained, "I realize that I am a stranger to you, but I assure you that I have received vaccination for the virus, and I am definitely as healthy as a horse!"

Emily smiled shyly. "Sure. That would be lovely. My name is Emily..." she held her hand out to him, and they shook hands.

"Emily. What a beautiful name. I am Darian." He glanced at his table and back to her, "just give me a minute to grab my drink and to notify our waiter." Darian was thrilled, *Man, oh man, this is my lucky day! To have the supreme opportunity to dine with such a beautiful woman!*

Emily smiled while she watched him scamper to his table and back to her. She congratulated herself. *Works every single time! I don't even need to change my script!*

Once seated, he said, "I must confess, I had noticed you from my table, and that you seemed to have been stood up." He paused. "Not any of my business, of course."

Emily smiled. "Ah, so you are here to rescue me?" She gave a flirtatious laugh and continued, "Oh, what a chivalrous man you are! And handsome, too!" She looked down for a moment, seemingly embarrassed. "It does appear I've been dumped."

With that, Darian melted. "Oh, it happens to us all at one time or another. It's their loss." Kindly, he offered, "Let this dinner be my treat, a nice surprise after all."

She smiled while looking directly into his eyes. "Thank you," she said with a whisper.

They continued with light conversation. *Like putty in my hand*, she assured herself.

In the course of eating their meal, Emily shared that she was indeed single, with no attachments; and she was successful in a current business venture. Darian indicated that he too, was available and had quite a portfolio of successful investments.

Wow, she's smart and successful, too! How could I be so blessed?

"Please tell me, Emily, about your business venture. How are recent economic troubles affecting you and your business? I have been more cautious lately in today's climate, but I remain always open to possibilities."

Emily raised her hand to get the waiter's attention. Once he arrived at the table, she said, "The food was superb."

"Shall I remove your plate?"

She nodded. Darian quickly dropped his utensils onto his plate. "Yes, everything was delicious. Please clear the table."

The waiter asked, "Is there anything else I can get you? Drinks? Dessert?"

Darian glanced at Emily, who shook her head. "No, not at this time."

After the waiter had left, Emily proceeded to provide an overview of a 'tried and true' get-rich scheme. She enthusiastically used drawings that she scribbled on a napkin with descriptions of marketing language she had learned while dabbling with a few network marketing companies. She included testimonials and her definition of residual and passive income. She eloquently gave her entire pitch perfectly.

Emily ended with, "Of course, your initial investment of ten grand will grow wealth exponentially, especially as you continue investing. This is all short-term! You can expect to gain a two-hundred percent profit within a few months. No product to sell – just investment growth."

Darian was intrigued with Emily while he looked into her beautiful eyes, full of excitement over having the privilege, the opportunity to be her total focus. He decided, against his better judgement, that he would consider donating the initial investment, and see where it goes.

Still, he asked, "Emily, I'm not familiar with this business venture, but this sounds like it could be a pyramid scheme. Is it legal?"

Emily smiled and gently grasped his hand. "I promise you that this is not a pyramid scheme. You can absolutely trust me. I am the most honest person you will ever meet." She continued to smile while holding his gaze with her eyes.

Darian was hooked, and she knew it. She pulled out her cell phone.

"Oh, look at the time. I have lost track because you are so interesting!" She gave him her best seductive grin, what she referred to as 'the closer,' and concluded, "I must be going soon...so what are your thoughts, Darian? Are we going to partner together?"

Darian asked, "Partner together? How frequently do we meet?"

He was mesmerized with the thought of partnering with her, of developing a relationship with this dazzling, intelligent woman.

Enthusiastically, Emily exclaimed while she tightly grasped Darian's hand, "Oh, honey – we'll be spending lots of time together from now on!"

While deep in the clouds of Darian's mind there were warning bells going off inside, he chose to ignore them; he did not want to take the chance that he may not see her again. In this state of mind, he heard himself say, "Oh, well, I don't usually do this...but yes, I want in. I can put in the initial investment right now if you'd like..."

"Perfect, Darian!" Under the table, she quickly pulled the front of her dress lower, and seductively leaned in toward him, revealing much more cleavage. With her other hand still grasping his hand, she seductively ran her hand up his arm to his shoulder.

She whispered in a throaty voice, "I so want to build a tight relationship with you. We can work together..."

Darian felt drunk with her seduction and the wine, and quickly whipped out his checkbook.

"Okay, my beautiful one, what did you say? Ten grand?" Eager to impress her beyond that of any of her other business partners, he added, "How about double that?"

Emily was so excited with her accomplishment in this deal that she jumped from her seat to hug him close while he sat like a deer in the headlights. She managed to rub her breast against his shoulder while she breathed into his ear, "Yes, Darian, oh, yes!"

Darian quickly wrote out the check, leaving the section 'payee' blank. He glanced up, "Who should I make it out to?"

Still standing beside him, Emily quickly reached for the check, answering, "Oh, I'll finish it for you." She motioned for the waiter to come to their table while she sat down. "Let's celebrate, shall we?"

Darian hardly noticed that Emily had quickly tucked his check away into her purse before the waiter had arrived at their table. He ordered a carafe of champagne.

Within only moments of waiting for the champagne, Emily excused herself, saying, "I need to go to the powder room, but I'll be right back."

She rubbed his shoulder as she passed his chair. Laughing inside, she thought, *See ya, sucker!*

Excited for a potential future together with this beautiful and successful woman, Darian received the champagne and took a few sips. Time passed without notice while he imagined their relationship growing exponentially in all directions, and he continued to sip champagne.

After another ten minutes, Darian continued to wait patiently, thinking, *Boy, oh boy, women sure take a long time...*

He glanced toward where she had disappeared to go to the ladies' room. He then fixed his eyes in that direction, as if he could 'will' her to come out. Slowly, his gaze lifted to the exit sign and he realized that the way to the ladies' room was also the direction for the exit.

He looked at his hands, remembering the last thing he had done... giving her that check. Sadly, he faced a moment of clarity.

Emily is not coming back. He put his face into his hands. *Oh God, what have I done?* He wanted to kick himself for being so foolish. *I even left the payee blank!*

Embarrassed and humiliated, but still with a shred of hope, he continued to sit at the table, sipping on the champagne.

About thirty minutes passed before Darian was fully willing to face the truth. He mentally beat himself up. *Look at what you did! You allowed this beautiful, flirtatious, seductive woman to sway your good judgement!* He looked at his glass in disgust, full of self-contempt. *And what about this booze you've been consuming? Man, you do know better than this...*

I've got to sober up, right now!

Darian motioned for the waiter and asked, "Could you please take the champagne away and bring me a slice of pie and coffee?"

The waiter removed the carafe and asked, "Which would you like, apple or banana cream pie?"

Darian ordered the apple pie with his coffee, which was swiftly brought back to him.

While Darian ate and drank his coffee, he began to feel himself regain his balance.

Whew. I look back on this now and I must realize: this woman, Emily – if that is her real name – had set out to defraud someone, and I had been selected. That means the entire scene was likely a set up; she probably wasn't even waiting for someone!

He allowed this assessment to sink in.

And, unfortunately, I think I was just one of many.

He continued to munch on his pie.

What should I do? Other people have been duped by her...others will be. I have no other choice, do I? I must go to the authorities. He shifted in his seat. *And...this will be very humiliating.* He ate the last bite and laughed., *And here I am, eating 'humble pie!'*

He realized: *I have no paperwork from her! And I gave this stranger a large check with the payee left blank. Oh, my. They will likely laugh in my face.*

He finished the coffee, paid his bill, and left a generous tip.

That night, Darian prayed:

"Dear Lord, I am grateful for the abundance you have given me, and I know that I am to be a good steward over my funds, to give generously to those in need as best I can. I have failed. Please forgive me for this terrible blunder, for allowing myself to be tricked. For letting money fall into the hands of a deceiver. Although I forgive this woman, Emily – whoever – and have no anger toward her, I feel the burden to alert the authorities. I want to do what is in my power to see that she cannot do this to another person. Once caught, she may feel conviction and repent of her ways. Please guide me, Lord. I pray for her soul. In Jesus' name, Amen."

The next morning, Darian did go into the local police precinct and filed his complaint.

The agent who was assigned informed Darian, "Sir, a woman of this description and mode of operation has been conning both wealthy men and women in Illinois, as well as in the surrounding states."

Darian responded, "Well, I'm not really surprised. She was smooth as silk."

The agent continued, "In light of these activities in a number of states, the Federal Bureau of Investigations is involved. I am actually an FBI agent assigned to this case."

Curious, Darian asked, "Do you have any leads?"

The agent confirmed this. "Darian, our investigations have revealed that a woman fitting her description stayed at the Villa D' Citta last night; using the same name, she has a plane ticket for Dallas, Texas. We have men at the airport to apprehend her as we speak."

"Wow" was all Darian could say.

The agent concluded, "Please stick around to identify this woman; it won't be long..."

While Darian waited, he felt the need to understand where Emily's point of view had come from.

He pulled out his iPhone and Googled 'love of money,' and found referenced 1 Timothy 6:6-10, 17-19, in the Passion Translation. He read that passage slowly:

'Loving money is the first step toward all kinds of trouble...

We have a "profit" that is greater than theirs – our holy awe of God!

To have merely our necessities is to have enough.

Isn't it true that our hands were empty when we came into the world, and when we leave this world, our hands will be empty again? Because of this, food and clothing are enough to make us content. But those who crave the wealth of this world slip into spiritual snares.

They become trapped by the troubles that come through their foolish and harmful desires, driven by greed and drowning in their own sinful pleasures.

And they take others down with them into their corruption and eventual destruction.

Loving money is the first step toward all kinds of trouble. Some people run after it so much that they have given up their faith. Craving more money pushes them away from the faith into error, compounding misery in their lives!

...To all the rich of this world, I command you not to be wrapped in thoughts of pride over your prosperity, or rely on your wealth, for your riches are unreliable and nothing compared to the living God. Trust instead in the one who has lavished upon us all good things, fulfilling our every need.

Remind the wealthy to be rich in good works of extravagant generosity, willing to share with others. This will provide a beautiful foundation for their lives and secure for them a great future, as they lay their hands upon the meaning of true life.'

Darian was truly sad for Emily.

Well, she has apparently chosen the position to take others down into corruption...for now. And I know I did the right thing to help keep her from harming others. But Lord, I know that You love her dearly, and You are a merciful God. I will continue to pray that she will decide to change from the dark path she is now on.

Two passages in Psalms come to mind as warnings while we make daily decisions. I personally find comfort in all of Psalm 37; that passage has brought me peace many times when I had found myself within a relationship with mean-spirited folks.

Though they plan evil against you, though they devise mischief, they will not succeed.

Psalm 21:11 Eastern Standard Version (ESV)

Be still before the Lord and wait patiently for Him; fret not yourself over the one who prospers in his way, over the man who carries out evil devices!

Refrain from anger and forsake wrath! Fret not yourself; it tends only to evil.

For the evildoers shall be cut off, but those who wait for the Lord shall inherit the land.

Psalm 37:7-9, Eastern Standard Version (ESV) (emphasis added)

Emily glared through the glass while standing in the line-up. She was furious that the FBI had been so dramatic in arresting her.

Handcuffs and reading my rights were excessive force! Especially in front of my wealthy oil man I had planned to fly to Dallas with! I only needed a few hours with him, maybe just the length of the flight! I could have been set for life!

She attempted to console herself. *Well, I always knew the chance was there that this day might come, but I am confident that I will find a way out...*

She pierced the glass with her angry eyes, wondering, *Who is responsible for this?*

Emily glanced at the other people in the line-up, thinking, *You are all losers! This is what you waste your time doing? Helping to nail folks like me?*

Indignantly she whispered, "I should not be here, to be treated like a criminal...those who fell for my tricks needed to be taught a lesson. They deserved what they got! They were left with plenty to get by on."

Emily fussed to herself. *I knew it, didn't I? At any moment one of my victims, probably that one from last night, Darryl, no Darian, would be so indignant as to report me.* She shook her head with disdain. *Stupid, stupid, stupid! I was too quick and reckless with those last few.*

Now what? Can I charm the court, the jury? What is my plan? What can I do to wiggle my way out of this mess?

Emily did not want to admit it to herself yet, but she felt alone. She was beginning to feel out of control, even desperate.

Then the idea came to her, *Maybe I can get Dad, or even Joe to pay the bail bond. Yes, of course! I just need to act as though I'm ... What? Remorseful, yea, that's it.*

She immediately changed her demeanor to display herself as a woman filled with humility, sadness, and remorse. She reassured herself, *Once they pay the bond, I will find my opportunity to leave the country, never to return...*

Filled with overwhelming regret, she whined in thought to herself, *If only I hadn't lived it up, if only I had had more time, I could have saved up a much larger nest egg to live on.*

THINGS TO PONDER

Becky and Emily lived in different circumstances during their childhood but were tempted in similar ways. How did they compare themselves to others? From comparing, what emotional path did they take? Was the love or want for money and better things ever quenched or satisfied?

Do you see that each woman had choices to make during every step of their journey? Sometimes it may not feel like there are choices, but do you agree that we do have control over our emotions, attitudes, and actions? Please describe where you saw examples of emotional override.

Were there instances in the storyline where you could see spiritual forces at work behind the scenes, both good and evil? Could you resonate with the apparent temptations and convictions that they had encountered?

The following verse appears to relate to Emily's current path.

In arrogance the wicked hotly pursue the poor;
let them be caught in the schemes that they have devised.
Psalm 10:2, English Standard Version (ESV)

What will become of Emily?

When temptation comes, are you alone in it? Which path will you take?

Seek His will in all you do, and He will show you which path to take.

Proverbs 3:6, New Living Translation (NLT) (emphasis added)

THREE

WHEN WILL JUSTICE PREVAIL?
SURROUNDING ISSUES OF SEXUAL ABUSE

ALANA IS A YOUNG, *beautiful woman who has been pursued by the male species for all of her life. She is filled with confused emotions; although she receives an enormous amount of attention, she appears to struggle alone, feeling unloved.*

"Hey, Alana, wait up!" yelled the high school's most popular senior football star as he waved his hand in the air and walked quickly toward her in the hallway.

Alana was excited to have his attention. *Oh! He does know my name! I wonder if he realizes that I have had a crush on him literally for over a year!* She smiled with hopefulness while she waited for him to catch up to her. *I wish I didn't have to wear this stupid mask, so he could see my smile!*

"Hi, Randy," she responded shyly.

I can't believe it! Randy wants to talk to me!

Randy came up close to Alana, touching her waist with his hand. "I'm having a party at my place this Friday night. Can you come?" He looked deep into her eyes, as if they already had a relationship.

She felt faint and could feel electricity running throughout her body, just from this one inappropriate touch.

"Oh, yes, Randy, that would be awesome!" she excitedly answered, without even noticing that she was automatically giving him a display of her large breasts while she swayed back and forth. As usual, her breasts were encased in a tight fitting, low-cut tank top. She noticed Randy's obvious and lingering stare at her cleavage.

Yep, Uncle Jim was right, my boobs are my greatest asset...the best way to get a guy's attention.

Randy slowly lifted his eyes back to her eyes and smiled lasciviously, licking his lips. "Nice... nice top you have there."

Alana swooned. *Oh, my God, I can't think!* She screamed inside to herself. *He is actually talking to me! Randy is so handsome!*

While she gazed into his eyes, she felt his hand slowly move from her waist to her butt, then he suddenly shoved her body toward him, at the same time thrusting his torso way too closely against her. Shocked and confused that he would be this aggressive after never speaking to her before this encounter, and with it being out in the open, Alana was frightened and felt helpless to do anything. She froze.

Suddenly, Randy let go, turned away, and walked on. Alana had to catch her balance and stood still while she watched him disappear.

Did I just imagine this? What just happened? She remained confused about the entire incident and wondered, *He didn't say what time or give me his address...Maybe he expected me to know? He probably has parties all the time. Maybe it was just some sort of joke to get my hopes up?*

I guess I'll just be ready for whenever, Alana told herself, not really believing he would approach her again, and not sure she should want him to.

Maybe if I'm not really invited, it's for the best? He is way too aggressive!

She walked toward the exit to go home, and as she passed a small group of girls, she overheard them giggling with sneak-peeks at her. She felt again the sting of humiliation.

Sadly, she admitted to herself, *I could never belong to that clique. Snobs!*

Alana had tried to join their little group last year, and their rejection was particularly painful. And then, soon afterwards her going all the way had become common knowledge.

Yeah, I thought Kenny loved me. He made me feel as if I did belong...for such a short time. But look what it got me! A reputation!

Once she and her first boyfriend, Kenny, had broken up, these girls spread sex stories about her to the rest of the school.

Okay, I know the stories probably came straight from Kenny's mouth, and are at least partly true. But it sure hurts that he had to broadcast our personal matters! We were making love in private, but when they talk about it, it sounds like it had just been dirty sex. A tear fell from her eye. *Okay, maybe to Kenny, that's all it was...*

Alana revisited the pain of rejection she had felt when her Kenny had abruptly dumped her. The whole relationship had been like a roller-coaster ride.

I tried to hold him off, to be a nice girl. And I did pretty good at that. Until...

Feeling overwhelmed, Alana sat in the empty chair in the foyer by the school's west-end exit door.

I still can't make sense of it. Did we really drink so much that I can't remember taking my clothes off? She rubbed her head while she remained confused. *One minute I was having fun and laughing with Kenny, and then he began kissing me and telling me he loved me. I felt warm inside, loved. Feeling kinda' faint, I had closed my eyes...*

And then, as if I had been asleep for a while...I awoke to see that he was pulling the zipper to his pants up, grinning from ear to ear. What? Pulling his zipper up? And I realized that I was laying down without any clothing on. What?

Alana remained confused, and – like every other time she attempted to revisit that incident – her head began to pound while she tried to figure out what had happened.

He told me I was the best 'piece' he had ever had, gave me my clothes, and urged me to get dressed because we had to leave. I remember wondering, 'How could I have been his best when I don't even remember doing it with him at all?'

After that first encounter, Kenny suddenly had an enormous interest in making love with Alana often, and he knew her body intimately.

Recalling her past experience, she reminded herself, *He knew my body even more intimately than Uncle Jim. He visited my bed often while he lived in our home...financial troubles, he had told my dad, but he told me he was there just for me...from the time I was twelve until I was fourteen years old. He had said he loved me. But his kind of love hurt, and then he left.*

Well, Kenny left me after only two months for another girl! I did everything I could to keep him, but I guess I just was not sexy enough.

Alana had enjoyed their time alone together more than she could explain or understand. Even now, she continued to long for his affection and the closeness they had shared. She asked herself, *That was love, wasn't it?*

Very slowly she began to understand that to her, his physical contact had meant love; but to him, it meant conquest. Even while coming to this realization, she continued to believe, *I know that he really enjoyed being with me! I was just not enough to keep him happy!* Perplexed, she blasted herself, *What more could I have done?*

Alana decided not to think about what happened that first night with Kenny anymore. She admitted to herself, *I know he is the one who spread those stories...just forget him, Alana!*

Alana took a moment to seriously look at herself. She knew, at least subconsciously, that she is a beautiful girl in a fabulous woman's body: with big pale blue eyes, long and shiny black hair, plump lips and curves any red-blooded male would want to use as their playground.

Alana realized that boys and men alike appeared to experience a sexual arousal whenever they were around her. *Strange, but I love the attention!* she told herself.

But I need... I want more than that. A relationship! Uncle Jim and Kenny both told me that they loved me! Is it so wrong for me to make myself look better, to enhance my appearance for them? Is it wrong to please someone who says that they love me?

Alana confessed to herself, *I was completely powerless to say no to their physical advances.* She felt the sting of shame. *Did I really want the sex? No, I'm just starving for love and attention.* She allowed another tear to fall while she wondered, *Why am I never enough for a relationship?*

Alana! She fussed at herself, *You have got to be smarter than this! You could get a disease, or even pregnant!*

She bitterly remembered her parent's reaction when she was caught last month kissing and petting with her dad's friend while in his new convertible. *I had only agreed to go for a ride!* She had explained to them, *What girl would have refused that opportunity?* But her parents blamed her for the incident. Alana felt her heart break with her mother's cruel words, *Mom called me ugly names... a whore! and said I will wind up pregnant before I graduate!*

It's unfortunate, but some children are not nurtured, encouraged, or protected from harm by their parents or other adults. Alana appears to be terribly confused about sexual abuses she has suffered alone. Could these signs of confusion and faintness be forms of learned dissociation? Those same responses may be misunderstood by others; for example, her lack of response or remaining frozen instead of (verbally or through body motions) telling her assailant to stop or giving verbal approval.

What does the Word of God say about her parents' treatment toward her?

Fathers, do not provoke your children to anger [do not exasperate them to the point of resentment with demands that are trivial or unreasonable or humiliating or abusive; nor by showing favoritism or indifference to any of them], but bring them up [tenderly, with lovingkindness] in the discipline and instruction of the Lord.
Ephesians 6:4, Amplified Bible (AMP)

Alana awoke in the hospital alarmed that she had tubes with fluids and a monitor hooked up to her. She struggled to scream 'what happened?' but no one was in the room. She looked at her still body before her wondering, *Is everything still here?* She gently moved her arms and legs, and with some relief, she wondered, *Was I in an accident?*

The nurse came in and noticed that Alana was conscious. The nurse asked, "Honey, can you tell me your name?"

"Alana," she responded.

"Do you know where you are?" The nurse checked Alana's vitals while questioning her.

"Yeah," Alana answered, noticing the nurse's name tag and stethoscope. "I'm in the hospital, but I don't know why. Was I in an accident? Are Mom and Dad okay?"

The nurse clenched her jaw. "Honey, you were attacked. You have suffered some injuries, and you've been unconscious for two days." She regretted having to tell this girl such horrific news, and the nurse quickly added, "You have tested negative of the virus or of any STDs..."

"Attacked? STDs? What happened?" Alana asked with shock and confusion.

She tried to raise up, but the movement caused her neck to begin shooting pain to her head. She muttered, "Am I okay?"

The nurse bit her tongue, sorry that she added the bit about sexually transmitted diseases to a girl who did not yet realize she had been raped. She explained, "I'm sorry, that's all I'm at liberty to say. Your doctor and your parents will be in to see you shortly, and they will help you with any of your questions."

This empty response brought anxiety and fear to Alana; she urgently pleaded with the nurse, "Please tell me...what's wrong with me? What happened?" She waited for an answer, but the nurse turned away. While the nurse disappeared out the door and into the hall, Alana shouted after her, "Why can't you tell me what's wrong?"

Alana was panic-stricken and her head throbbed. Her desperate thoughts were interrupted when her doctor and parents rushed into the room. She listened while the doctor indicated that she had been attacked, raped, and that she suffered several minor contusions and lacerations. Their primary concern had been that she was unconscious, suffering a concussion from head trauma.

Alana struggled to process what they were telling her. *What? Someone hit me hard enough to knock me out? Who could do this? I don't have any enemies, do I? And, was I raped?*

Alana's mother came to the bedside and grabbed Alana's hand. Squeezing it, she said, "I was so frightened for you, Alana! I've been praying for you the whole time!"

Her father, too, came to the opposite bedside, and gently kissed Alana's forehead. Tears welled up in his eyes, causing Alana to feel sad that she had caused them worry.

Her father prayed aloud, "Oh, God! Thank You for bringing my precious daughter back. Please forgive me for not taking good care of my Alana, my precious gift from You. Help me, Lord, to help her with a much better life from now on. Keep her healthy and strong..." He began to sob with relief that she was awake.

Immediately after Alana's father had finished his short prayer, two police officers, who had been cordially waiting in the doorway, walked into the room. They introduced themselves and asked to speak with Alana alone.

One of the officers asked Alana, "Can we ask you some questions about what happened to you?"

Alana answered sheepishly, "I will tell you what I can."

There was a discussion among the officers and her parents. Her mother insisted, "We should stay. She's a minor, so we don't have to allow you to speak with her alone!" Getting herself riled up, she shook her head. "We want to hear what she has to say!"

Calmly, the female officer explained, "We mean no disrespect...but we have found that a teenager, especially a young lady who has been attacked in this manner, may not feel free to talk openly with their parents' listening in. Not at this point, anyway." She paused for effect. "Would you please allow us to proceed with our questions, and then we can better conduct our investigation?"

Alana's father frowned. "Well, we don't want to impede progress." He turned to his wife and they whispered what appeared to be an argumentative conversation, with angry gestures and expressions.

They stood glaring into each other's eyes a moment, and her father reluctantly nodded his agreement to the officers; he then silently escorted his wife toward the door to the hallway.

Alana's father stopped, then turned and smiled at her, saying, "We'll be back soon, precious. Please answer these officers the best you can." Then, he blew a kiss, saw his daughter smile, and walked out.

"I love you, Dad!" Alana shouted after him.

The police officers reintroduced themselves to Alana and began to ask her a series of questions, which brought her already painful headache to a higher level with increased confusion.

Finding it hard to think about the questions being asked, she blurted out, "I'm sorry officers, but I don't know what happened, either..."

She sat up and composed herself, noticing they were writing down everything she said.

"You're asking me what happened on Friday night, but my last memory is of being in school...it was Wednesday, I remember, because I had just taken a test in math class. That's my last class, and then I was in the hall talking with friends, and I caught the bus home. That is all I remember, riding the bus toward home..."

"Wait. Was the bus in an accident? Why are you asking me about Friday, then? I don't understand!"

Her headache jumped up the scale to an unbearable level of pain.

The female officer explained, "Alana, records indicate that you were in school on Friday, then you went home. Your parents stated that you had told them you were invited to a party that evening. But they lost track of you at that point. They admitted to us earlier that they had been engaged in a heated argument, and failed to ask where the party was, or to notice you leaving. "So," the female officer emphasized, "They don't know where you went or to whose party you went." She waited for Alana's response, then continued, "Okay. If you don't remember Friday, do you happen to at least recall *where* the party was supposed to be, and *who* it was that had invited you?"

Alana remembered her excitement on Wednesday when Randy had invited her to a party on Friday. She remembered being confused and frightened when Randy had become suddenly aggressive in the school hallway.

Wait! Did Randy attack me? Oh, no...no, no...that can't be!

Alana began sobbing hysterically while she loudly and repeatedly babbled, "I need to talk to my doctor! I need to know what happened to me! Why can't I remember being at that party? Why? Why would anyone hurt me?"

The nurse walked back into the room, announcing, "I'm sorry folks. You will have to leave now. She needs her rest."

Reluctantly the officers gave up on questioning her any further and sauntered out of the room.

Desperately Alana kept asking these questions loudly into the air. "What happened to me? Who did it? Why can't I remember!"

Her nurse said calm, soothing words to her while she served Alana a glass of water and pills to take. Her nurse whispered, "Here, take these. This will ease your headache. You've had a busy day, and now you just need to rest..."

Alana had fitful sleep through the rest of that day and all night. She awoke the next morning feeling less pain and anxiety. After breakfast and the nurse had completed her rounds, she acquiesced to allowing both her parents to come into the room for a short visit, as long as they kept their masks on.

Her father squeezed Alana's hand and lovingly spoke to her with a tone of sincerity, "I have been praying for you all night, Alana. Thank the Lord that I have the opportunity to say this to you, my precious daughter." With this statement, Alana was fully alert to what he had to say next.

He held his breath a moment, slowly exhaling as he began, "I have failed you in so many ways, Alana, and for that, I'm tremendously sorry. I hope that someday you can forgive me." He wiped tears from his eyes.

Both Alana and her mother looked at him confused, not knowing what he could be talking about. Seeing how distraught her father was, Alana quietly tried to console him. "Dad, you are a good father...I have no clue what you're talking about."

He held her close, as he finished his confession, "I've got to get this off of my chest, sweetie, please let me continue." He blew his nose into a tissue from the bedside table and straightened himself up for his heart-wrenching speech. "Your mother took over with raising you from the beginning, and I allowed that. Even to the point of giving up on bringing you to church so you could learn about the Lord..."

He looked up as if he were facing the heavens. "Lord, help me through this." He continued, "And, until the other night, I knew nothing about your accusations regarding your Uncle Jimmy, but I did have a feeling something wasn't right about him being in our home, and I did nothing. I said nothing. I'm so ashamed." Emotionally he shouted out, "I believe you, Alana, my precious, innocent daughter. I love you, and I believe *you*."

Alana began to weep quietly while she listened. She muttered to herself, "Always, Dad...I always wanted to hear this..."

"What happened to you is because I failed to protect you as your father. That is a betrayal. Alana, I promise you that I will spend the rest of my life making it up to you, my precious daughter."

After saying this, he and Alana hugged while they sobbed uncontrollably. Her mother looked on, confused and irritated while she silently remained in denial that her brother had done anything wrong. Alana's mother continued her on-going pattern of denial thoughts used to assure herself, *My own daughter! A flirtatious little tramp was lying about my brother! Even if he did do anything, she must have asked for it, chased after him! Or, he was drunk, or on pills. Whatever may have happened, it was* not *his fault!*

What seemed like an hour of various simultaneous emotions bouncing around in the room was actually only minutes. Alana and her dad pulled themselves out of their tears and smiled, beaming at each other.

"This is my dad," Alana murmured, knowing a new beginning had just blossomed.

Can you empathize with Alana's confusion and upset with several simultaneous emotions? Although she received the answer to her prayers for her father's love and support, her ongoing pain of rejection from her mother remained. It is upsetting in and of itself to not be able to recall the details surrounding a physical attack; but through the investigative questions, Alana realized that she likely had been viciously attacked by a fellow classmate, and maybe even by her own heartthrob, Randy, the ever-popular football star. She could not understand why that would happen.

We do not see the details of the legal process that Alana underwent in these pages, or the raw emotions she must have endured as she became more fully aware of the levels of betrayal she had experienced by her mother and fellow classmates. With the support of her father, Alana did file charges against her Uncle Jimmy, an offense which was still within statutory limits for the rape of a minor.

For several reasons, Alana's attorney had advised against filing charges against Alana's ex-boyfriend, Kenny. Her attorney doubted the court's relief for several reasons, which included:

- *There was no evidence that the initial sexual acts were forced, especially since she continued a relationship with him; and*

- *There were photos that seemingly proved her sexual relationship with Kenny had been consensual between two minors of the same age.*

Luckily, neither Alana nor Kenny faced charges for the distributed photos, which were claimed to have been distributed by accident.

A witness revealed that Randy and other football players had planned their rape and attack of Alana. Alana did press charges against Randy and other classmates who were involved in the gang rape she had experienced. Since she remained unable to remember the events leading up to and including that attack, charges were based upon evidence obtained through investigation and the witness who had come forward.

How many of us would have looked at Alana, a very sexy, yet naïve woman-child, and judged her for the way she dressed and pursued attention?

Unfortunately, many young girls are misunderstood as they chase after much needed love and attention; they realize the male species is attracted when they dress provocatively and when they behave promiscuously. Sadly, some such young girls are destined to receive notice from society's dark corners, where pedophiles and lascivious young men await.

In hindsight, with the help of her father and through study of the Word of God, Alana sees warnings to heed. Her desire is to help other girls to avoid the snares she has fallen into.

"Be sober [well balanced and self-disciplined], be alert and cautious at all times. That enemy of yours, the devil, prowls around like a roaring lion [fiercely hungry], seeking someone to devour."
1 Peter 5:8, Amplified Bible (AMP)

~

Alana awakened to the churning of her stomach in the early morning, something that happened often lately. She would wake up hungry!

Well, I'm eating for two now...

She was thankful that at least she no longer suffered from morning sickness.

"This is just practice, right my precious? You will be getting me up early for breakfast for many months once you're born." She patted her tummy lovingly, adding, "And your Momma will love doing it, too, my little angel!"

Alana allowed herself to look back at the horrible arguments she had with her mother once her parents became aware of her pregnancy. Her mother pushed hard for an abortion, saying, "You'd be stupid to keep the baby of a rapist! Was it really rape? Why would you then want his baby?"

Alana answered with a firm resolve, "This is a life in me, a miracle from God regardless of the horrible things I've gone through." She explained further, "Besides, my baby did nothing wrong. She is innocent! I will do nothing to harm her!"

Alana's father offered her continued support regardless of what her decision might be, but he could not resist offering his own feelings about it. He calmly shared, "Two wrongs don't ever make a right. Alana, please do not destroy an innocent life because someone else committed a crime against you." In everything he said, he included his unconditional support, "Remember Alana, I am with you in this. I will support you in any way I can." Alana remembered her solid decision, vowing, "I will *not* end my baby's life. Whatever else happened in my life, this is the good thing: she *is* my gift from God."

That would only make her mother furious, even to the point of screaming. She threatened, "If you won't get rid of it, then you'd better put it up for adoption! I am *not* going to raise that baby." Finally, she screamed, "You can leave!"

Alana loved to remember that her father physically stepped in, saying, "Alana, what I said in the hospital is true. I'm on your side."

The room became so quiet, you could hear a pin drop. He looked at his wife with disdain, daring her to speak again.

"With the toxicity in this house right now, I'm inclined to set you up immediately into an environment somewhere peaceful, like in a nice Christian place for unwed mothers until the baby is born." He paused, then added, "Does that sound appealing to you at all, Alana?"

Alana nodded agreement; this is exactly what she had planned to do herself.

He had glared at his wife so she would remain silent and said, "While you're there, I will have time to make changes in your mother's and my arrangements...."

Alana had instinctively known what he meant. She had watched her own pain in the home, as well as his with her raging mother always in the forefront.

His wife gasped and asked, "You mean, divorce? After all these years that I've put up with you?"

"Yes, dear, I'm afraid it is long overdue." He deliberately shifted his attention toward Alana, and smiled tearfully at his daughter, "Your mother and I both betrayed you already, by not protecting you from harm. I will never betray you again."

He took Alana's hand in his.

"My plan, only if you are agreeable to it, is to find a suitable duplex or house with a grandfather suite where you, your baby, and I can live together, for as long as you wish." He looked at Alana to find approval. "I believe that can work out for both of us, at least until the baby is older and you have another good plan. What do you think?"

Alana was elated with the idea, but out of respect for her mother she held her feelings at bay.

"Yes, Dad, I like that idea. And I am absolutely fine with going to an unwed mother's home for a while. I have so much to think about..." She glanced at her mother, who was quietly smoldering, and Alana added, "I need to be in a peaceful environment for my baby's sake."

Alana felt the baby kicking inside her, taking her from her memories. "Whew," she said to her tummy, "thank goodness we are here, little one – in a peaceful place!"

Alana realized she had essentially lost her mother for a while. *Hopefully not forever,* she reminded herself. *Maybe, once she sees her precious granddaughter, she may change her attitude. I hope so,* Alana thought, hugging her stomach.

She smiled, remembering how her father had come through for her.

Speaking to her tummy, Alana affirmed lovingly, "Little sweetheart, my dad brought me to this nice home for unwed mothers because he wants me – us – to always live in peace.

She thought to herself, *And while we're here, he is faced with the chore of handling division of property, belongings, and legal matters with Mom. I am so thankful not to be involved in all of that...*

While at the home, Alana was learning from the Word of God; learning about the love of God over her life. She hoped that someday her mother could understand, but she realized that everyone has free will to make their own decisions, good, bad, ugly, or indifferent.

She hadn't been there but a few days before a counselor had led her to the Lord for forgiveness of her past sins and she accepted Jesus as her Lord and Savior. Every time she thought about that defining moment, she broke out in praise and gratitude.

"Thank you, Lord, for Your grace in Jesus Christ!"

Knowing that everything she had done in her past was now erased, her gratitude motivated her to live the best Christian life she could.

"I will serve You, Lord, all of my life!"

Alana was finally feeling that her life had purpose, and she had faith that she was never alone.

She often prayed, "Dear Jesus, I'm so excited and honored to be loved so much by You, that You would grant me the responsibility of caring for a helpless little baby, my child. Thank You for my life, for my baby! I will always praise You!"

Alana looked outside of her bedroom window of the St. Anne's Home for Unwed Mothers, appreciating the beautiful scenery of the courtyard below.

"Thank You, Lord, for another beautiful day!" she said with sincere appreciation.

She knew to be thankful for every moment she and her unborn baby had on earth. What seemed to be the most dreadful thing to happen to her — to be the victim of violence, become pregnant, and wind up in this home — was actually an awesome second chance for her.

Her thoughts were interrupted when the staff at St. Anne's announced that the group session was about to start.

The group counselor, Dr. Wren announced to the circle of young women in the small classroom, "Today is a special treat for us all. Alana has agreed, for this, her first time, to give her story of years as a sexual abuse victim, leading her to where she is now. It's her testimony of how the Lord brought her through horrible circumstances." Dr. Wren rested her eyes upon each of the girls before stating, "This is proof again that what the enemy means for harm or for evil, God always has a good plan for your life!"[1]

Dr. Wren explained to the group of young women, "You are all here through your choice, your decision not to terminate your pregnancy. And we will work with you during your pregnancy." She shifted the pages in front of her and continued. "God gave people free will, a huge gift, with the ability of us to decide things for ourselves regarding any matter, even whether to come to Him or not."

Dr. Wren cleared her throat, "Similarly, this organization respects and honors your decisions. You came here after already opting not to abort your baby. Now the only remaining choices are whether you keep it or adopt it out. We only give information, support, and prayer. No pressures!"

"Not always, but with this group in particular, you have each found yourselves pregnant through no intentional acts of your own. Your decision in whether to have sex or become pregnant was taken from you. If you share any details of your personal story, that is of your choosing; again, no pressures."

The counselor opened her Bible. "Before we get started, let me emphasize where those aggressive, lustful actions taken against each of you came from. I'm getting my support from the Word of God."

"I'm reading from the gospel of Mark[2], Jesus is speaking to the Pharisees and teachers of law:

"'It is what comes from inside that defiles them. For from within, out of a person's heart, that evil thoughts come – sexual immorality, theft, murder, adultery, greed, malice, deceit, lewdness, envy, slander, arrogance and folly. All these evils come from inside and defile a person.'"

One of the girls timidly asked, "so when we talk about what's inside, we're talking about what a person is thinking and wanting to do?"

Dr. Wren nodded her head, saying, "Yes, and so much more than that. When we chose to allow ourselves to continue along that path, then we take on behaviors, attitudes, what we talk about, and finally the decision to launch that evilness into action."

She looked around the room to see if the girls were understanding her.

"Each of you here today has been a victim to someone else's aggressive, lustful, and violent actions. Your attacker or your abuser had allowed their heart and mind to be defiled and had consciously decided to harm you.

"I know each of your personal stories. None of you set out to participate in an adult sexual act, none of you wanted to have sex, but it was forced upon you. Each of you were too young, too inexperienced, and too vulnerable to have made any decision to participate in that evil action. Don't put the blame on yourselves!"

Dr. Wren knew that these young women had been blamed for their misfortune; they blamed themselves, too.

She assured them, "You may have been a victim of someone else's wickedness in your past, but you are no longer in that harsh, dangerous, and toxic environment. The Lord loves you and has a good future planned for you."

There were shouts of encouragement among the girls, and they settled down to listen to their friend, Alana.

Dr. Wren smiled at the girls, then she nodded for Alana to begin her story.

"Yes," Alana admitted, "I became sexually active at twelve years old. At first, it was forced on me, and it really hurt. But when I realized I could do nothing about it, I learned to get through it, and then over the years, Uncle Jim influenced me to see it as a normal thing, and as a part of love. He encouraged me to believe I was just on earth to please him, or to serve other men."

One of the girls asked, "Alana, did you ever tell anyone about what your uncle Jim was doing during those two years?"

Alana responded, "I tried to talk with my mother about it one time, but as soon as she realized that I was accusing Uncle Jim of raping me, she wouldn't let me finish talking. She had glared right through me, pointed her finger in my face, and shouted, 'Not *my* brother! You're a liar!'"

Alana looked sadly down at her hands for a moment, knowing she had never faced it before, "My mother failed me." She added, "My father didn't know what Uncle Jimmy did. And yet, years later when he did find out about it, he's the one who carried remorse for not protecting me."

One of the girls in the class added, "My mother didn't believe me either... she sided with her boyfriend. Then she threw me out."

Dr. Wren expressed, "I wish you had known! There are resources available for victims of sexual abuse. For starters, you could contact The National Sexual Assault Hotline number:1-800-656-4673 or go to RAINN.org."

Dr. Wren announced a short break, because she could see that Alana's story was already very emotionally personal to a few of the girls there. They too had tried to get help in their situation, but whoever they had approached had refused to admit or face that the abuse was going on. Some had been accused of lying or causing the rape to happen. Like Alana, their abuse had continued, and in that they were being taught through actions that there was no way out of the situation. They learned to believe the sexual abuse experienced was okay, to be expected, *even* that it was a part of love.

After the break, the entire group of girls felt more empowered, and they encouraged Alana to continue with her story. She told about her two-month relationship with her boyfriend, Kenny, a sexual relationship that began with unwelcomed sex.

"Why did you stay in it, Alana?" Dr. Wren asked.

Alana sighed, explaining, "I had been taught that it was what a girl had to do, there was no way out of it, and I believed it was causing him to love me... or to care more about me."

Other girls resonated with that explanation. Some of the girls admitted that their first sexual experience with their boyfriend had not been wanted, but they stayed with him anyway because they thought that they needed that boyfriend's love and attention.

Dr. Wren spoke gently, "But now we all know that's not true, right?" She looked around the circle, with every girl nodding in agreement.

She continued, "It was men or boys giving in to their lustful nature to the detriment of a female, their victim. When a person forces themselves on another person, sexually, it is a crime of rape. Love is not in that at all, but violence is."

Alana confessed, "The dumbest thing I ever did was to think Randy, the school's football star, had a real interest in me."

Filled with curiosity, everyone waited quietly for Alana to continue.

"I believe that I went to the party, of course thinking there would be several guys and girls there. Probably, they explained that the girls were running late. I have no idea because my memory of that night never came back. And while I waited, they apparently slipped me a date-rape drug in the one beer I had. I know that much from the toxicology report."

Each girl in the group leaned in, eager to hear more. Alana began giving details she had learned through the investigation and in court.

"I learned that it was four guys, including Randy. All were on the football team, and I was merely entertainment. Once I had been drugged, they took turns raping me. Later I started coming around fighting, while others held me down. Incriminating photos were extracted from a few iPhones, also used in court..."

A couple of the girls began crying because their experiences had been similar in that they were forced to have sex with one or more unwanted partners and hearing about it brought those memories to the present. Dr. Wren asked Alana to pause for a moment while she immediately dealt with these girls' upset.

After a few minutes had passed, the girls agreed that getting their emotions out was good for them, and they were able to continue listening. Most of all, they wanted to be supportive for Alana and for each other.

Alana continued, "The rape continued through the night and into the early morning hours. Jeff, also a football star, arrived around 3:00 am. But when he heard and saw all that was happening, he wanted no part of it. He tried to reason with Randy and the other three football players, to put a stop to it, but they would not listen to him."

Alana stopped to take a sip of water. She cleared her throat and continued.

"Jeff had already slipped out to call the police when someone hit me in the head with something. He didn't know who it was that hit me, or with what."

Alana glanced at Dr. Wren, hoping she would help her tell her story.

The counselor nodded in agreement and interjected, "Apparently, Jeff contacted the police just in time, because you were unconscious when the police and ambulance arrived. Who knows what might have happened if they had not arrived when they did? Maybe those boys would have killed you."

Dr. Wren looked at each of the girls in the group saying, "I believe it was no accident that Jeff came to this party — it was in response to the Lord's prompting! His courage to do what's right, despite strong peer pressure, might have literally saved her life!" She continued, "In life, we're presented with choices: to do good, or to do evil. And with each choice we will find related rewards or consequences."

"Really," one of the girls added, "we see consequences of jail-time for these rapists!"

Girls began to cheer. The counselor interrupted, "Alright, alright... settle down, now..."

After the room became silent, a girl asked, "Alana, did you get any disease or virus from the guys at that party?"

Alana smiled, saying, "Well, that is one thing I was assured of before I even realized I had been raped. A nurse told me I tested negative for viruses and for any STDs...Thank you, Jesus!"

Another girl asked, "Alana, is one of your rapists the baby's father?"

Sheepishly Alana responded, "Yes. Randy was determined to be the father. As part of his plea agreement, he will not be in pursuit of custody or visitation rights as the child's father... at least, that is true for now. I'll keep my prayers up for that."

The counselor added, "Since Alana is a minor, it was statutory rape in all of the cases with those who were also minors. Her uncle Jim faced appropriate charges that fall upon an adult who was found to have raped a minor. He made allocution, or a formal statement to the court in order to receive fewer years. There were settlements in each case, so Alana has not had to testify in court." She paused. "All faced charges and incarceration time, including, they are registered as sex offenders. I believe Alana may still have the right to bring them to civil court at another time."

One of the older girls confessed, "I was the entertainment for the senior football stars while I was a sophomore, but I didn't have the guts to come forward with it. My reputation was ruined, and I couldn't handle it. I quit school. You are so brave!"

The group of girls agreed unanimously that Alana was indeed courageous; they clapped their hands to congratulate Alana for sharing with them.

Another girl asked, "I just don't understand why a man would attack a young girl, or why a group of guys would attack a fellow classmate like that. Were they so desperately in need for sex that they had to take it?"

Dr. Wren explained, "Sexual lust may have been a small part of it, but they had allowed themselves to be overcome with evilness. The rape itself was not about sex, but about control over another person, about mercilessly joining in with comrades, and most of all it was about the individual decision to be violent. They desired and enjoyed harming another person, that's where their 'lust' was."

Alana waited until they had quieted. "I blamed myself for remaining in that terrible relationship with my Uncle Jim, and then with Kenny. I blamed myself for dressing sexy in front of Randy, classmates, and everyone. I blamed myself for not being able to do anything when I was being touched inappropriately. So many reasons to blame myself!"

She paused. "Regardless what blame I carried, I have repented of it all and accepted Jesus as my Lord and Savior. He paid the price for any blame I may have had. Now, all of my past sins are gone."

She hugged her tummy. "I have no reason at all to feel lonely or unloved. Jesus is always with me, my dad has become an integral part of my life support, and I am blessed with my precious baby...a miracle!"

Their counselor rested her hand on Alana's shoulder and said in a serious tone, "Alana, regarding the blame game, I'm not saying you were void of any responsibility, but you had been trained by the lack of interest and love in your childhood home and by the wickedness of men and boys to perform and behave as you did."

The other girls listened intently, knowing this applied to them as well.

She changed position and continued, "But now, because you are a believer, a follower of Jesus, whatever blame you may have had in it, although I believe you were a victim, it is gone through His grace, by the blood of Jesus Christ. You are washed clean, hallelujah!"[3]

The girls stood up and the room was filled with cheers and clapping.

Dr. Wren continued, "You're not even eighteen yet, but I see a woman before me who is wise, with a strong testimony to share. Your testimony will bring many girls to the Lord for healing and hope for their future. You will evoke change."

Alana beamed. Finally, she felt love and contentment. She knew, just as surely as God had already given her baby purpose from the time before entering her womb, that she herself had a calling in life. [4]

She let this sink in, and noted, *I know with certainty that my purpose in life surely does include sharing my testimony with other young women of the Lord's deliverance. If He rescued me, He will do it for others!*

She remembered that defining moment when she had turned to God for forgiveness and accepted Jesus as her Lord and Savior. Filled with praise and gratitude, she quickly exclaimed, "Thank you Lord for *Your grace* in Jesus Christ!"[5]

Suddenly, Alana announced, "I am going to name my little girl Grace!"

THINGS TO PONDER

Has this story brought you encouragement to empathize with and pray for young women who appear to dress provocatively and behave promiscuously for attention and love? Are there ways you could offer positive support and influence?

Have you ever stood by uninvolved while someone you should care about is being mistreated or abused? Can you see how Alana's mother was emotionally abusive because she was habitually toxic and non-supportive? Can you relate to the guilt and conviction that Alana's father felt? If so, can you come to the Lord about it like Alana's father did?

Time and time again, Alana's inaction to fight off the sexual advances of her predators were misinterpreted by both the predators and on-lookers. But isn't it plausible in such instances, that those symptoms of dizziness, confusion, or difficulty in thinking could be signs of dissociation (detachment) as a result of previous incidents?

Which of these characters decided to stand with their armor on? What armor could you visualize? If you were to continue this storyline, how would it end for Alana's mother, Uncle Jim, Randy, and his fellow attackers? Would you hope for their repentance and coming to Jesus?

Do you have circumstances in your life where you may be wondering: when will justice prevail? I recommend calling out to the Lord in prayer and to wait in patient faith for His justice, that will happen in His perfect timing and in His perfect way.

FOUR

WHAT WILL BE YOUR LEGACY?
LASTING EFFECTS OF EXPOSURE TO ABUSE

THE SETTING BEGINS in rural Kentucky several decades ago, at a time and place where man is king and all others are his subjects; male chauvinism was the norm. We have a young couple, and each partner comes from a life of violence, uncertainty, and child abuse within broken homes. Not sure what a loving relationship should look like or how to achieve it, they married and are raising their young child. The marriage had failed from the onset, but they limped along, forming a dreadful pattern of domestic violence.

To add to the weight on an already rocky marriage, with economic struggles, his work hours remained light and inconsistent. Already, some bills were falling short. Her meager income as a waitress at the local restaurant was keeping them afloat, but with that came grave resentment from him.

Cathy grew more and more afraid while her husband, Frank, prowled around the living room like an angry caged wolf.

She surmised, *Here he is, working up his rage again. What's new?*

As appeared to be his favorite practice, being the bully that he was, he roamed through the house shirtless, randomly snapping his belt in hand. In disgust mixed with fear, she knew, *Even when without his belt or other weapons—a knife, gun, or whatever else he could use as a club—Frank is much taller, heavier, and stronger than than me; after all, I am only 5'2" and 100 pounds soaking wet. Where's the challenge in attacking me? I am certainly no match for him in a physical fight.* She admitted to herself, *I don't know when the next smack with the belt will happen, or what else may be in store for me.*

She shook her head. *I just don't understand it! Why can't he just appreciate me? I work twenty-four, seven: waitressing, clean the house, cook, take care of Daniel, and do my wifely duties...but he just grows more and more vicious. Frank doesn't even resemble the man I fell in love with.*

A partially-memorized passage came to mind. *I remember the scripture, 1 Peter 5:8, about the Devil prowling around like an angry, roaring lion, looking for who he could devour.*

She watched Frank glare at her from across the room and whispered to herself, "I am looking at the Devil right here in this room!"

This time, Cathy was especially afraid because she had felt compelled to be honest with him that she wanted a divorce. She remembered sharing with him a few days ago, "I cannot take the abuse anymore! I won't..."

She had some of the many reasons on the tip of her tongue, but she didn't dare breathe them; it would be accusatory and would bring his hot revenge on her. But she whispered in her heart, *Frank's feelings for me were proven by the multiple times he strayed. He strayed with married women, and even with women who had a bad reputation! But he refused my affections.*

Just reviewing it in her mind now brought her humiliation. *Everyone knows about Frank running around on me, but that's okay! Nobody knows about the abuses at home or would care if they did know. How can they look at his indiscretions and unkind remarks and find it acceptable behavior — even to laugh about it?*

In disgust, she fussed at herself, *His crude and hateful buddies mock him if they ever catch him treating me kindly.*

Cathy remembered when she had fallen out of love for Frank; she wanted to remember it now to affirm her resolve while he continued to pace the floor like a wild animal, working himself up for his next attack.

She recalled, *It was last fall, on our ninth anniversary, and he had promised to take me out to eat. Stupidly, I had allowed myself to be excited with hopeful anticipation because he had only taken me out to a restaurant twice in our whole life together. I had saved up for that day to get my hair done up and I put on the nicest dress I had. When Frank came home, instead of being impressed, he became angry at the very sight of me. There was no love, only contempt.*

She had ignored his anger, excusing it to a bad day at work.

And I still believed that once he was out with me that he would enjoy celebrating our time together at dinner. Maybe the fire we once had when we first met would rekindle? I still had hope!

She admitted, *I was disappointed that he did not choose to appreciate my hair and clothes. Frank did not wear anything nice. But I managed to brush all that with excuses for him.*

After we dropped my precious Daniel off to the babysitter and we were back in the truck alone, Frank turned to me...

Cathy began to cry, but made herself revisit it all.

Frank turned to me and angrily bellowed, "Where in the hell do you want to go!"

I heard the intensity of his harsh words, I saw his horrible scowl...the truth hit me in the face. This man does not care about me at all.

Cathy could envision the change within herself that had occurred during that one event.

Wasn't it immediate? My heart closed up toward him. In that instant, my heart had grown cold. She remembered calmly responding, *"Nowhere. Nowhere at all."*

To me, our marriage had ended; our divorce had just happened.

That memory brought her to the very dark blemish in her life that had happened only a few short months after her desolate anniversary.

She acknowledged, *Yeah, I was vulnerable. I was like an innocent lamb ready for slaughter. Sweet ol' Carl, my charming supervisor at that horrible factory...every day at work, he dressed up in his nice outfits, oozing with kindness, always attentive, and so excessively empathetic when he noticed bruises on me. Carl was also a vicious wolf, well-experienced in pouncing on unhappy and abused women. I was such a fool!*

Cathy felt like punching herself for her stupidity.

I thought we were going to meet to talk, hug, maybe even kiss. I did not even realize we would have sex! It was awful but I didn't refuse! I felt nothing! And yet, it did happen, I committed adultery...

Feeling that familiar overwhelm of self-loathing and shame, Cathy asked herself, *Will I ever feel like God forgives me? Will I always feel dirty?*

She admitted, *Through those actions, I lost a good-paying job. I have allowed this horrible man in front of me now to abuse me all the more because of my own guilt, like I deserve no better treatment.*

Sadly, Cathy then visited a better time that had happened a few years ago, when Daniel was only five years old on that momentous spring day that she had turned her life over to the Lord.

I was so happy in Jesus! I went a long time full of joy, even while still in this terrible marriage. Regretfully, she asked herself, *What happened to me?*

But she knew: *I let the struggles and violence of this failed marriage take my focus, and my eyes were no longer on Jesus...*

Frank suddenly screamed obscenities at her, breaking Cathy from her thoughts.

While Cathy watched Frank slapping the belt on the coffee table, she wished she had listened to the wise women at work who had advised, "Never tell the man ahead of time that you're leaving. Get your stuff, the kids, and run!"

Cathy berated herself, *She had even suggested I make an escape plan, but I ignored her. Stupid!*

But, Cathy reasoned, *careful pre-planning had seemed wrong and deceitful to me. I wanted to be up-front and honest about it.*

She now fully realized the mistake she had made. She considered, *Frank has never hit Daniel, so my son might come out of this awful situation alright, but will I make it out alive?*

Desperately, she searched her mind for options.

Because Frank is clearly more agitated than usual, and because most of the abuse happened after Daniel was asleep, maybe I will be safe if I sneak into Daniel's room this one time and pretend to be asleep in the bunk bed below his?

Cathy weighed the possible danger in doing this. *But I just don't see what else I can do to find safety. Not this time.*

She quietly tip-toed into Daniel's room and slipped into the empty bed.

Surely, Frank will not come in here, she thought. *Surely, I will be safe in here...*

But to her horror, Frank did come in, jerked the covers off, and snapped her with his belt. The instant pain was excruciating, but Cathy remained silent and still. Before she had recovered from that, with one fisted grasp, Frank ripped her gown off, all the while

Cathy laid still, as if she were dead. Cathy's mind and body were screaming in every direction, but prayerfully, her solid resolve was this: *I will play possum through all of this, no matter what may happen...*

Frank punched her a few times, but she remained immoveable. He stood by the bedside, quietly hovering over her.

I can sense his presence! I can feel his hot breath on me! But I will remain as if dead.

Finally, he left the room. Cathy laid still all night.

Oh, God! Let us live through this night! I am so thankful that at least Daniel did not have to hear or witness any of this, I'm so thankful he's still asleep through it all!

She constantly assured herself they would be safe through the night, and she believed that Daniel was asleep because he, too, remained motionless all night.

Fortunately for Cathy, Frank was expected to show up for a union meeting to find out if his local factory might go back to work full-time or if the plant may shut down.

Cathy recalled, *Frank told me yesterday that he anticipates it to be an all-day event! Surely he will go to it, and we can leave while he's gone!*

Cathy could hear Frank stomping around in their bedroom, and then in the kitchen. But this time, Cathy did not get up to fix his lunch; she remained in the bed as if dead.

Frank jerked Daniel's bedroom door open and bolted into the bedroom, yelling, "I'm having to make my own damn lunch, you bitch! When I get home, you had better be gone or I'll kill you!" Igniting his own fiery anger, he yelled, "Do you hear me? I mean it!" He stomped out, slamming the bedroom door behind him so hard she could hear the hinges rattle.

Cathy realized, *Daniel surely must be awake now. How much did he hear? All of it?* She and her son both remained motionless in their separate beds.

Once they could hear the front door shut and the sound of the truck engine could be heard while it traveled away, Daniel, not even eight years old yet, jumped up. With red eyes from fright and lack of sleep all night, he said to his mother in the most serious, adult tone, "Mom, we've got to get you out of here."

Cathy saw the wisdom in his words and agreed. She thought, *After all this time I had believed I had to stay for his sake. 'No matter what, you must always stay for the kids,' is what I always heard...but they were wrong. I was wrong. Look at my son...he witnessed all this mess and now he is having to lead me out of this hell himself!*

Cathy knew that she and Daniel could be in danger if Frank should suddenly decide to come back.

"Son, we need to get dressed, and then we'll pack a few things we will need for a little trip. Okay? We'll be fine."

Quickly, Cathy decided that it was clothes they needed most and gathered what clothing they had for the both of them. All the while, she was amazed at how little she and Daniel had.

Cathy noted to herself, *Here and now, at least where we live, the man of the house deserves special food choices, fishing gear, guns, and boats. But look at this,* She fussed to herself in stark disbelief, thinking, *Only two trash bags full of clothes — mere rags — is all we really have worth taking! Why didn't I notice this vast disparity before?*

Cathy peered out the living room window to ensure the truck was not in sight. She grabbed the keys to her little 1974 baby blue Ford hatchback from her pants pocket and tentatively stepped out the front door. Cathy looked around, and once she felt safe, she motioned for Daniel to come with her.

"Come on, Daniel, I'm going to treat you to breakfast!"

Cathy nervously glanced back and mustered up some hope.

I will try to get Daniel's bunk beds and our other belongings later...

Did you know that the most dangerous point in a domestic violence situation is when the woman (statistically, it is usually the woman who is the victim) tries to leave her abuser? If you, my dear reader, need to know critical information on how to safely get out of your dangerous or toxic environment, please contact experts in this matter for information and help:

If it is an emergency, dial 911
The National Domestic Violence Hotline number is 1-800-799-7233
(SAFE)

It is through this national number and your local women's shelter where you can talk with experts for a safe escape plan. If you have any issues at all relating to domestic violence, I urge you to find out what resources are near you and reach out to them for information now. It could be a matter of life or death, or injury to you or your children. Please, do not wait until that one last time you expect yourself to tolerate the abuse, that one ultimate blow-out that makes you run. It literally could be too late!

It makes no sense to wait until the situation escalates.

We see a variety of choices Cathy and her husband have made to bring them to this dangerous juncture. Apparently, for a time, Cathy was wearing her full armor of God; her focus was on the Lord. During that time, she remained in peace regardless of her surroundings. But betrayals, violence, and temptations distracted her. Can you resonate with that?

At the time of this horrific incident that caused Cathy and Daniel to flee their home, Cathy had been a waitress at a local family restaurant. She was scheduled for work that same day they had left the house.

Cathy brought Daniel with her to the restaurant, knowing her boss would find a place for him to eat while she struggled to figure out where they should go or what they should do. Cathy had offered a white lie to her boss, mumbling, "Sorry about bringing Daniel to work with me, but my sitter had an emergency to come up. Once Daniel's finished eating, I'll have arranged another sitter."

Well, at least we're safely out of the house. But I can't think of what to do next! What if Frank thinks to come here to take Daniel? Should I tell my boss of possible danger? Should we go to a shelter?

Cathy remained emotional and confused; she decided to confess it all to her boss, thinking, *My boss is so smart and collected, she will know what I should do. Besides, she needs to know in case Frank shows up at this restaurant and makes a scene.*

Cathy stopped her boss, who was walking by while taking her morning inventory, asking, "Dorothy? Could you sit and talk with me for a few minutes? I need to tell you something..."

Dorothy knew about Cathy's ongoing troubles with Frank; she had figured since Daniel was with Cathy something had happened.

"Sure, Cathy, I have time right now."

She sat down with Cathy, looking at Daniel from across the room and then at Cathy's sad, blood-shot eyes.

"Cathy, I'm not going to beat around the bush. I didn't believe your sitter-story. So tell me, what's *really* going on?"

Hesitantly, Cathy began telling her, "Well, I had a rough night with my husband. Daniel may have heard and seen some of the ugliness, I'm not sure how much of it. But this morning, Frank told me...he threatened to kill me if I didn't leave."

Dorothy saw that Cathy's eyes were tearing up and quickly grabbed a tissue from a nearby box; she handed it to Cathy. Cathy dabbed at her eyes and blew her nose while tears fell.

She continued, "Daniel and I grabbed some clothes and left. I had to tell you because I don't know what Frank may do. I'm not sure what to do next. Can you help talk me through this?"

Dorothy patted Cathy's hand on the table and reassured her with soothing, kind words. Then, she responded, "Honey, it was only a matter of time before it came to this. My idea is for you not to worry about work today. When Daniel is finished with his breakfast, take him to my house. Frank doesn't know where I live. You both will be safe there."

She watched Cathy composing herself while she reached into her apron pocket, retrieving her house key. "Here, take this, go to my house. You and Daniel rest. Then tonight, when I get home, we will brain-storm and figure out your next steps together. Okay?"

Cathy sheepishly accepted the key and agreed with Dorothy's plan. She chatted with Daniel until he had finished his breakfast, and they quietly left the restaurant. Again, Cathy was cautious while they walked through the parking lot to her car, and she looked back several times while driving.

She surmised, *I don't think anyone is following us, but just in case, I'd better add a few extra street turns to be sure.*

On the way to Dorothy's house, Cathy realized Daniel wasn't partic-ipating with her in the non-stop friendly chatter. She attempted to explain, "Sweetie, Dorothy has invited us to stay at her house for a while so we can rest. Are you tired?"

Daniel nodded that he was.

"Okay, I'm tired, too. I'll put you to bed for a nice nap, and then this evening, after we're well rested, we can talk. And I'll answer any questions you might have. How's that?"

Daniel looked out the window while he quietly responded, "Okay."

Inside Dorothy's house, Cathy took Daniel to what she determined to be the guest bedroom and tucked him into the queen sized bed. He immediately fell asleep. Cathy gently smoothed the hair on his head.

"Everything will be alright, my little man. I promise you."

Then, she quietly crept out of the room, shut off the overhead light, and pulled the door closed.

Exhausted herself, she found a nice recliner to sit in with the intentions to think about what they might do, but instead, she fell fast asleep.

That evening, Dorothy and her husband came in the front door with a ready-fixed meal from the restaurant. The sounds of the door startled both Cathy and Daniel, and they each walked from where they were into the kitchen to greet Dorothy and her husband, who were already setting the table for dinner.

After dinner and the table had been cleared, the adults sat back at the table, encouraging Daniel to go watch television. Daniel turned the television on, but came back and set himself leaning against the wall opposite the dining area so he could hear all that they said.

Dorothy began the conversation, "The plan seems simple! While Daniel is on summer break from school anyway, I've been able to arrange a babysitter — one who we can all trust — to come to my home and watch him during the day while the rest of us are out. Is that okay with you, Cathy?"

Cathy appreciated Dorothy's tenacity and agreed.

"Cathy, you need to find a good divorce attorney and get a custody and separation agreement started. We might know of some resources from church. And, you need to begin hunting for an apartment." Dorothy stopped and then pointed out, "There's no rush on that, we know it may take three weeks or so to find a good, affordable apartment."

Cathy readily agreed.

Dorothy's husband interjected, "I think Cathy should hide her hatchback in our garage for these few weeks and ride to and from work with one of us."

"Good idea!" Dorothy agreed. "What do you think, Cathy?"

"Oh, yes, I like that idea. I felt I needed to be very careful getting here, and I was a little worried I could be followed."

Dorothy announced, "Well, that's enough for us to do for now. Down the road, once you have an apartment, we'll find out if you can get your belongings. If not — through our church connections, we have a woman in mind who can provide some free furnishings if needed. No reason to think that far into the future right now."

Cathy expressed her gratitude for their help profusely.

What are your thoughts on the arrangements Cathy has made thus far? It might appear staying with a friend with an anonymous address might seem safe. But, how hard would it be for Frank to find out where Cathy and Daniel are? Shelters tend to be much safer for women and their children to stay in with domestic violence cases because the location is not shared or known and there is no viable connection of that shelter to be made with their temporary residents. Therefore, friends and family of the victims are kept from harm's way as much as is feasible.

What are your thoughts on what Daniel, an eight-year-old, has seen and heard within a toxic environment? Does anyone seem to be fully aware of his need to have questions answered and assurances made regarding his future?

By the third week, Cathy was able to find a small apartment, and with co-workers' help, she paid a deposit on it. But that apartment was not furnished; they would be moving into a completely bare apartment.

She pondered, *If only I can get a few things from the house that we need...do we dare try it?*

Cathy posed this question to Dorothy, her husband, and a few co-workers within a gathering at Dorothy's dining room table (again, Daniel was able to listen to this adult conversation from the opposite wall).

Discussions went around within the group, and two potential volunteers emerged for helping her retrieve some of her belongings. Two kind and brave co-workers agreed to help Cathy gather a small truckload of only essentially needed belongings from the house, including Daniel's bunk beds.

To avoid conflict, and knowing there may be danger in it, they decided to do this at a time they could reasonably count on Frank not to be at home. Cathy explained the situation to her boss and friends.

"Frank routinely goes fishing early every Friday morning with his friends to the lake, which is several miles away. Usually, he doesn't get home until late, or he will stay over through the weekend." She paused for a moment. "But I haven't seen him now for three weeks, so I'm not sure if his schedule is the same." Suddenly feeling a burst of guilt for asking this of her co-workers, she blurted, "Maybe we should forget this idea. Frank has been a violent man in the past, not just with me, but with other men who were in arguments with him. Maybe this stuff isn't worth it!"

But her co-workers took this as a macho-man challenge, determined more than ever to get the job done.

One of them thought, *Hey, I work out at the gym all the time. I'm sure I can overthrow this good ol' boy. I could come out a hero!*

The other co-worker, who was already a bit of a daredevil with his car racing tricks, imagined, *Oh, finally! An exciting, maybe dangerous adventure! Like on TV!*

They discussed the terrain: Cathy's home was isolated in a valley, next to a creek, facing a narrow and winding roadway with miles of woods behind the house; innately, there was risk just by the location and having only one means for entry and exit.

One of the two co-workers who had volunteered asked, "What if he suspects you'll be coming by for things from the house? What if he and his friends are lying in wait for us? We could be caught up in a trap and get hurt. Maybe we should bring weapons?"

Quickly, Dorothy's husband announced, "There will be no weapons brought to that house! That's a good way for things to escalate, and you could get into serious legal trouble." He added, "If you feel the need for weapons, drop the idea now."

The other co-worker (the one who was eager for the thrill of danger) suggested, "I agree, there is a certain amount of risk, but someone can be on standby to call the police if anyone shows up. We can go in cautiously, with intent to only grab a few necessities, and quickly leave. Quick, in and out."

Cathy's boss, Dorothy agreed, "Yes, that sounds reasonably safe. Otherwise, Cathy and her son may not get any of their belongings." She rubbed her forehead thoughtfully, and added, "I realize Frank has been vicious with Cathy on many occasions, but for the most part, it's isolated to domestic violence with her, not her son or others. We have no reason to think he would attack strangers, especially if we are only attempting to get specific things that belong to Cathy and her son — certainly nothing that belongs to him."

Dorothy's husband qualified what and who the standby should be, proclaiming, "I will be the lookout, sitting on the opposite side of the road before the mouth of the driveway. If I see anyone come in after you, I'll immediately call the police."

The first volunteers restated their agreement.

"It's agreed then: tomorrow morning, seven o'clock, you," said one of the volunteers, pointing at Dorothy's husband, "will be parked inconspicuously across the street from the mouth of the driveway as the lookout and you will call the police if anyone other than us goes into the driveway while we're still there." He paused for a moment while everyone at the table nodded agreement. "Then, we quickly go in and out, only getting the bunk beds and a couple of necessities of yours and Daniel's. Right?"

Cathy nodded, and all agreed to the plan.

Cathy was excited and nervous at the same time, anxious for the ordeal to be behind her so she could set up their apartment for their first night in it. She didn't discuss the matter with Daniel, other than to generally indicate they would be moving soon into an apartment with some of their belongings.

Cathy assured herself, *Daniel doesn't need to fret about any of this; the less he knows, the better.*

Early Friday morning, with Dorothy's husband stationed along the road nearby, Cathy and her two volunteers cautiously approached the house on the narrow driveway since they saw no sign of Frank's truck being there. As planned, they allowed themselves only fifteen minutes to rush inside the home and grab the bunk beds. While the truck was loaded with those beds and a few other belongings, Cathy and friends began to drive out.

Suddenly, a large truck roared through the narrow roadway and parked very close to their smaller truck, blocking their passage. Other trucks arrived.

Frank and his fishing friends jumped out of their vehicles and ran to the small truck. Cathy and her co-workers were terrified, especially at the sight of Ted, the most ruthless looking of all Frank's buddies, who was equipped with a shotgun.

Cathy and her friends were helplessly captive to an angry and potentially violent group of men who were yelling and cursing at them. Ted jerked open the small truck's passenger door, grabbed Cathy, pulling her out of the vehicle with one hand while still holding his shotgun with the other. All stood still and watched while Frank grabbed a crowbar from his truck, ran over to where Cathy stood, and swung it at Cathy's head; at the last moment, she ducked. Barely missing his target, Frank tried again, but at the last second, Dick, Frank's oldest and smartest friend, grabbed the end of the crowbar and blocked him just before he could make the kill.

Almost immediately after that, the state police car arrived. Two troopers began to question individuals at the scene. The volunteer who had been eager for risk was especially relieved for the police officers' arrival.

Ultimately, the trooper in charge required Cathy and her friends to leave without anything. They were each thankful to be alive and glad they were allowed to escape without harm or arrest.

Cathy was filled with regret and remorse, thinking, *I risked these nice young men's lives for stuff! Our stuff is so not worth the risk of lives.*

Once others at work became aware of what had happened, Cathy's bosses and co-workers collected bedding that was sufficient to make sleeping bags for Cathy and Daniel to spend their first night on the bare floors of the empty apartment.

They all arrived at the apartment with the bedding and set it up in the two bedrooms. Then, they had pizza picnic-style on the living room floor. Everyone acted cheery and told cute jokes. Laughter filled the room.

Cathy did not share with Daniel how she and her friends had just survived a violent, life-threatening incident. But of course, he was aware that she had gone to get their things and came back with nothing. While tucking Daniel into his sleeping bag on the floor, Cathy attempted to be vague about the incident.

"Daniel, you know I meant to get your beds and some of our things today, but it just didn't happen the way we had wanted. Anyway, please don't worry about a thing! Tomorrow, a very nice old woman from out in the country plans to give us beds, and any other furniture we may need. You and I can help pick them out! Won't that be fun?"

She watched her son, who did not say much of anything lately. She attempted to encourage him. "This setup is just for tonight. Bedding on the floor is like we are camping. That's not so bad, right, son?"

She hugged Daniel and fluffed his hair while he shrugged and looked away.

Cathy kissed her child goodnight in his hand-made sleeping bag, saying, "Your daddy and I both love you very much. This problem is only between the two of us, not you. Remember, Daniel: tomorrow you will have a nice bed to sleep on, and this apartment will look great." She hesitated, sending up a silent prayer before adding, "You will see, all will be fine."

Later, Cathy thought about Daniel's quietness.

Although Daniel appeared to be upset that we did not have our belongings and beds, he did not complain. Cathy decided her assurances had satisfied his anxiety. *He just needs some time to adjust, that's all.* Silently, Cathy thanked the Lord. *I'm just relieved and grateful that we came out of that incident alive. Thank You, Jesus, for sparing us!*

Late that same night, Cathy was awakened by a loud knocking on the door. Genuinely terrified, she timidly answered the shouts through the door.

Has Frank found me? she wondered.

A stranger shouted to her, "Do you know where your son is?"

She responded, "Yes, he's in bed..."

"You sure of that?" bellowed the stranger on the other side of the door.

Quickly, Cathy checked on her son.

Oh, my God! He's not here!

She opened the door, with a sudden mixture of emotions: fear, courage, anger.

She demanded, "What happened? Where is my son?"

The stern, dangerous-looking man calmly turned and motioned for his buddy to get Cathy's son out of his car and brought him to the door. She immediately grabbed her son inside. Just in case they thought they could come inside as well, she blocked the entrance with her body.

The huge stranger said, "Ma'am, I don't know what's going on here, but we found your son a half-mile away, deliberately jumping into traffic."

In shock, Cathy was unable to speak.

The apparent good Samaritan continued, "He said something about his dad hating him so much that he wouldn't even let him have his own bed to sleep on."

Cathy sadly nodded, "We're going through a nasty divorce. But I will have beds for us right away." She paused, then added, "Thank you for saving my son!"

He tipped his hat; he and his men left.

Cathy slowly shut the door, shocked that Daniel had been that upset without her realizing it, shocked that he had apparently attempted suicide... and at such a young age.

What do I say to him now? How can I help him get past this? Lord, please help me!

Cathy prayed over her son and told him repeatedly that she loved him, that his daddy loved him, too. But Daniel didn't say anything; his eyes were blank while he looked over at the wall in his bare room.

When adults struggle with domestic violence or separation drama, extreme and dangerous tempers may ignite suddenly; the adults involved are likely not paying attention to what the children may be witnessing or feeling. They are suffering emotionally from the toxic and volatile environment they are in!

If aware or in the midst of the chaos or violence, those children will make assumptions about themselves. Usually, the children who are caught in the middle will see themselves as the reason for the troubles; somehow, they will feel that it was their fault for the failed relationship, for the violence, and for the injuries or death. The children likely feel rejected and unloved by one or both parents.

If children are part of the domestic violence environment, it is imperative that you have an escape plan that does not bring the children to a safety risk or even to witness anything that is unpleasant or violent.

What if Cathy had already gone to receive expert advice at a local shelter before Frank had any idea she planned to leave? Could Cathy have done anything differently to avoid much of the trauma? When leaving their home, could they have gone to a shelter where experts were available to offer resources and temporary shelter and counseling?

More importantly, Cathy had access to The One who wanted her to turn to Him for help, The One who has ultimate control, but with the distractions of what was in front of her, sadly, she did not focus her attentions on the Lord.

~

The psychiatrist, Doctor Pendergast, smiled at his emergency patient and offered his hand.

"Hi, I'm Dr. Pendergast. Come in and have a seat so we can chat a few minutes." He motioned for Cathy to sit at the sofa.

"Thank you, sir," she responded while she nervously looked around the room while the doctor shut the door.

"What is your name, young lady?"

"I'm Cathy. Cathy Saunders," she said, nervously clasping her hands.

"So, your boss and fellow employees are worried about you. That's why your boss and coworker brought you here today." He paused, then asked "Can you tell me if anything has happened to you recently? Maybe it was yesterday, or last night?"

Cathy blurted, "I did the best I could this morning! I don't know why my boss felt the need to bring me here!" She stared into space before finally answering. "Yeah. Yesterday my ex-husband, Frank, was supposed to meet me to drop off my son, Daniel; but they were not there. I waited for over an hour! Then I thought he must've been confused, so I went home — to my apartment and called him."

Cathy began crying and sniffing. She grabbed a tissue the doctor held out for her.

"Frank laughed! He said I will never see Daniel again!" She began wringing the tissue frantically. "Frank laughed, and kept saying everything is his! My home, my belongings, the money, and Daniel!

"I begged Frank to give him back to me, but he just kept laughing! He sounded like the Devil himself! Then, he hung up on me."

Cathy broke down with sobs.

After allowing Cathy to cry it out for a few minutes, Dr. Pendergast asked, "Cathy, did you call your lawyer about it?"

"Yes. He said that since we had no signed custody or settlement agreement yet, Frank — my ex — didn't legally have to give him to me."

"What did you do next?"

"I called the police, but they said their hands were tied, this was a custody matter. I called my lawyer back, but he did not answer. I called Frank back, but he did not answer. I called one after the other over and over...the whole time, in my mind, I could hear Frank laughing!"

"That must have been horrible, Cathy. What did you do then?"

"I'm not sure. I remember looking into the living room mirror, where the phone is, while I was calling, and I saw myself screaming."

The doctor made notes in his notepad, then asked, "Can you recall how long that lasted?"

"No. The next thing I knew, it was very dark in the room, and I heard myself still screaming. The phone was still in my hand. I don't know what happened next. I must've gone to bed."

"What did you do the next day, this morning?"

"I went to work."

"To work...where is that and what do you do?"

"I am a waitress at Dorothy's restaurant." Cathy looked at the doctor. "But you already know that. You've met my boss."

Dr. Pendergast nodded and said, "Yes, I do. You have friends at your job who care, and they are very concerned about you. Did they tell you why they were concerned?"

Cathy nodded. "Yes. One of our regular customers came to me with a question and I couldn't remember his name."

"Was that the only concern they had?"

"No. My boss, Dorothy, told me on the way here that the phone had been ringing all morning — it was my turn to man the phone — and I never picked it up." Cathy looked confused, "But I didn't hear it ring at all."

Dr. Pendergast came over to the sofa to sit beside Cathy and grasped her hand.

"Cathy, I'm going to ask you a serious question, and you must answer me, okay?"

Cathy nodded agreement.

He cleared his throat and asked, "Cathy, if you never see your son again, will you survive?"

Cathy sadly shook her head no, answering, "I don't know...I don't know."

"You must decide now, one way or the other. I'm not going to pressure you to say yes or no, but I want you to be sincere about it. So, I'll ask you again." He paused. "If you never see your son again, will you live?"

Again, Cathy shook her head. "I don't know..."

Dr. Pendergast squeezed Cathy's hand. "Cathy. Please look at me, and answer this final question: if you never see your son again, will you live?"

Something inside Cathy stirred, and she softly responded, "Yes."

With her positive response, the confusion and clouds in her mind began to dissipate. She began to feel clarity in her mind.

Dr. Pendergast smiled and patted Cathy on the shoulder. "I'm so glad you have made the decision to live. You need to survive, to thrive. Whatever happens in this world, you will need to be able to survive and to thrive."

Cathy nodded agreement, with a renewed desire to live and to make it through this horrible nightmare. She realized that she was barely holding on. Someday, she hoped to be whole, for Daniel's sake.

Someday, I will get to see my son again and he will be okay...oh, God, please let him be alright!

Gaining strength in her resolve, she vowed to herself, *And Daniel will eventually see his momma as a successful, thriving woman who has overcome!*

Dr. Pendergast marked boxes on his chart and looked up.

"I think you will have the strength to make it, Cathy, no matter what. Let us make an appointment for you to see me again in a few days so we can chat. I also want to write you a prescription... nothing strong, just to help you relax." He emphasized, "You will need to start on your prescription today."

He studied Cathy for a moment, then asked, "I'm curious, would you feel better to take a few days off from work, or would you rather continue working through this?"

Cathy looked apprehensive. "Do I have a choice? I would rather work. That seems to be the only thing I have right now. When I'm busy, I don't have time to think about my troubles."

Dr. Pendergast nodded his head. "Yes, and you have people there who genuinely care about you. I agree." He added, "But if at any time you feel overwhelmed at work, let me know, okay?"

Cathy nodded agreement.

"So, how do you feel right now compared to how you felt when you first came in?"

Cathy considered his question. "Well, all of this morning, really, I felt like I was in a dream. I was very confused and lost."

"And now, how do you feel?"

Cathy was surprised to realize the change. "I feel like I just woke up. I can think again. I think I have hope."

"Good, Cathy! That's what I wanted to hear!"

Dr. Pendergast wrote out and gave Cathy her prescription and a reminder for the next appointment.

"Now, Cathy, your friends are in the waiting room to take you back to work or home. Your choice." He added while offering his hand, "It was good meeting you."

Cathy smiled while she shook his hand, "Thank you, doctor."

Have you ever fallen into such miserable calamity that you felt confused, unable to think clearly, and there was no hope in you? Were you on the edge of a nervous breakdown?

A good counselor, psychologist, or psychiatrist is trained to draw you out of it before you sink into a debilitating depression. If you feel yourself with any such symptoms, please reach out to professionals for help.

In addition, if only circumstances could have permitted it, the child would have benefited from much-needed counseling. A child's mind and emotions could not have handled the domestic violence environment. The child is a victim, too, as a witness to vicious brutality, whether verbally, physically, or both. Certainly, if a child acts out in any way (here, apparent suicide attempt), they need professional help.

Over and over again in the Word of God, we learn that the Lord is our protection, rescue, comfort, and deliverance in times of trouble! We have examples that follow (all using the New International Version (NIV)):

- *Psalm 63:7: Because you are my help, I sing in the shadow of your wings.*
- *Psalm 36:7: How priceless is your unfailing love, O God! People take refuge in the shadow of your wings.*
- *Psalm 46:1: God is our refuge and strength, an ever-present help in trouble.*
- *And, like David cried out to the Lord while King Saul chased after him to kill him, we too can cry out to the Lord as in: Psalm 57:1 (emphasis added): Have mercy on me, my God, have mercy on me, for in You I take refuge. I will take refuge in the shadow of Your wings until the disaster has passed.*

I love passages that refer to us being able to run and hide in the shadow of our Heavenly Father's wings; there we find peace, comfort, and security.

~

It was as if they were celebrating a big fishing event in Frank's living room while dividing up Cathy's belongings among Frank's buddies, sharing beers all around to celebrate their support. Frank entertained the group while he bragged to them (again) about how he was able to run Cathy off with nothing, especially because he took Daniel from her. They all laughed along with him.

Daniel was alone in his dark bedroom, crying for his mother throughout the night, wishing that he could not hear what the laughter and bragging was about.

Dick said, "Surely she knew you had connections with the folks at the courthouse? She was some kind of stupid to leave you!"

"Yea, she was always nothing but a stupid bitch." The laughter continued.

Dick happened to think of a possible issue. "What did you tell your son? Surely he wondered what happened..."

Frank quickly responded, "Oh, I have that covered! I told him that his mother doesn't love him anymore and she left us for another man!"

Ted, who was hard-hearted and who had experienced divorce warned, "You might want to run that story to the school, too, just in case she tries to see him there."

"Oh, hell no! He is mine!" As a side-thought, Frank said, "Thanks, Ted, for thinking of that!"

They continued to divide many years' worth of Cathy's belongings among themselves — spoils of their conquest. They drank beers late into the night. Drinking and celebrating was a pattern they always followed before and after each fishing expedition.

How do friends and family members play a part toward the continuation of abuse within a family?

- *Subtle ways may be to say or do nothing as they hear of the* abuse or witness it, which may be interpreted by the abuser as designated approval.

- Are there any children watching and listening to indirect or direct approval of the abuse?
- Reasons and excuses for violent or malicious behavior may be used to mask the issue.
- Gossip and lies spread about the victim are used to justify the abuser's actions.
- A more aggressive choice may be to enjoy benefiting from the spoils of the abuse while offering words or actions of encouragement — even to join in on the plots and plans.

If family and friends personally take on abusive actions, regardless of how small their part is against the victim(s), they then essentially become participants in the abuse!

Are you concerned that the legacy of abuse within your family may continue? What can you do differently?

I encourage you to read A New Song Rises Up! *by Carin Jayne Casey. It includes my testimony about a life of abuse (child abuse, life-threatening domestic violence, and abuse by toxic people), what I learned from those experiences, and how the Lord delivered me from them all.*

Indeed, if the Lord rescued and redeemed me, an undeserving sinner, He will do it for you!

~

Months after the divorce, Cathy remained heartbroken with the court's decision to give full custody to Frank.

But it should have been no surprise to me! After all, he was the one with the money and power. I knew it, didn't I? He did have a friend in high places. She wondered, still carrying the heavy burden of guilt over her one horrible step into adultery, *Is this my punishment, my consequence because of that very brief affair I had fallen into?*

Cathy continually suffered over her horrendous sin and humbly turned to God for forgiveness repeatedly. She habitually went to church and knelt at the altar in repentance until one day, suddenly, the Lord dropped it into her heart that she had been forgiven from the first time she approached Him.

After that encounter with the Lord, she realized, *Of course He knew my heart, He knows everything! He knew I was sincerely sorry! He heard me from the first time I came to Him!*

The scriptures say that when we humbly come to the Lord with a contrite heart, fully repenting, then He forgives; and He forgets those sins!

Eager to prove this for herself, Cathy searched the Word of God about repentance and forgiveness. *Ah, I think this is my favorite:*

2 Chronicles 7:14. Cathy proceeded to recite this passage:

"Then if My people who are called by My name will humble them-selves and pray and seek My face and turn from their wicked ways, I will hear from heaven and will forgive their sins and restore their land."[1]

Cathy repeated the passage a few more times before she realized, *Oh, I know why this is my favorite! Because it says the Lord will restore my land. Maybe I lost it all in that situation, but I have hope for my future, happier life: maybe a wholesome relationship, a safe and secure home, and someday my precious Daniel will be restored to me as well. In the meantime, I need to keep patiently trusting the Lord, knowing that He is the one in control, not my enemies, and that He has a good plan for my life. Thank You, Jesus!*

The next step was to forgive herself, which she did after much more time had passed.

As a believer and follower of Jesus, I now have true hope. I can wait patiently for this temporary suffering to pass.

But as she said this, her heart remained broken, healing only in tiny increments. She reminded herself of what her pastor had told her: *I need to be patient with myself, too. Recovery is a process. Take one day at a time, one step at a time.*

Cathy recited from memory a special scripture that her pastor had introduced her to. She thumbed through the pages in her Bible and read it aloud.

Here it is, 1 Corinthians 10:13,

"No temptation has overtaken you except what is common to mankind. And God is faithful; He will not let you be tempted beyond what you can bear. But when you are tempted, He will also provide a way out so that you can endure it."[2]

Cathy assured herself, *Life is hard; but I will keep my personal vow to overcome while I continue to do the right things. I will not suffer more than I can bear. I will adapt. And if I can't endure it, my Heavenly Father will provide me a way of escape. This is true for my precious son, too!*

Good things do happen while you are in the midst of hard periods. And good things happened for Cathy while she waited to regain custody of Daniel. She was able to have visitation with her son every other weekend; it was always, a joyful reunion for them. Cathy met a kind and loving man who also loved Daniel as if he were his own son, and they married.

I heard a pastor say some time ago that in all of Job's sufferings, loss of family, friends, property, and health, his suffering was only for nine months. In the end, he was restored better than he had been before.

Suffering on Earth may be overwhelmingly painful while you are in the midst of it, but that suffering will not last forever. Haven't you experienced that, too? For instance, I suffered serious back pain and finally it was determined I must undergo major back surgery. Recovery involves very cumbersome and tedious steps; it took a year. I am now pain-free and fully-loaded with titanium. Do you have a story of suffering that includes recovery? Our suffering is only temporary, even as life on earth is temporary.

For His anger lasts only a moment, but His favor lasts a lifetime! Weeping may last through the night, but joy comes with the morning.

Psalm 30:5, New Living Translation (NLT)

∾

One day, Cathy's new husband, Bill came home with exciting news.

"Honey, I've been promoted! In three months, I will be supervising the whole region!"

Cathy was excited and proud of her husband's accomplishment until she realized it meant that they must move a three-hour distance from their present home so he would be near his new office.

Cathy's heart and mind flooded with anxiety and concern.

Three hours away! By the time I pick up Daniel it will be four, and how can I bring him to the house for only a long weekend visit? Our precious

time together is a struggle with Frank's many tricks, anyway...how, then,
is this going to work?

Cathy and Bill discussed how difficult it would be.

Her husband resolved, "We will find a way that we can do both. We just need the Lord's help to figure this out so we will continue visitation as it is with Daniel *and* move closer to the regional office."

Still anxious about it, Cathy suggested, "Let's keep this problem as our focus in prayers, every day and night until the Lord shows us the way."

They immediately began their frequent request in prayer to the Lord. Cathy's husband reminded her, "When two or three are gathered in prayer, in agreement, there the Lord is with them."[3]

While they prayed in the weeks to come, visitation remained an unnecessarily difficult ordeal. Once, Frank had told Daniel to wait for her, even though it was not her turn to get him. When she did get him at the scheduled time, this is when Cathy learned of this deceitful manipulation that only served to harm her child's sense of her love for him.

With the upset over the evil trickery of her ex, Cathy began again to fret and worry about their move. She cried out, "What will I do? Lord, please show me what I can do? We'll begin packing in days!"

Cathy tried to reason out a way by herself, even by researching the possibility of getting a helicopter license and renting a helicopter. She admitted to herself, *That idea is ridiculous! I can't afford the training, can't afford the rental. Besides, training takes time I don't have! I am seriously grasping at straws!* She broke down and cried. *How can I continue to see my son?*

Every time Cathy envisioned Daniel waiting for her, she could see his heartbreak. Her heart burned with anger toward Frank, but she determined to console herself, knowing that God does see everything that happens. She mulled the dilemma over in her mind.

The Devil certainly wants me to give up, but my Daniel and I would suffer great heartbreak. If I give into this absolute hatred that's brewing within me, I am giving in to the Devil. In fact, if I do not forgive, how can I hope for my sins to be forgiven? How can I hope for the Lord to help me with my present earnest requests to Him? I must forgive, for my own soul's sake. This I know...

Cathy took several deep breaths and put her hands together in prayer.

Dear Lord, I do forgive — help me to let it go! In Jesus' name!

When the time for visitation came, after she had moved far away from where her son lived, no answer from the Lord had come.

Desperately she pleaded, *What can I do, Lord?*

And in that same instant she saw her car in a new light; she realized that she could simply get into her car and drive the distance.

Yes. I guess the answer was in front of me all along. The mileage is extreme, especially considering the round-trip, but what else can I do? Quickly, she thanked the Lord that she had a reliable car, the time available, and the capability to drive it.

During her first long ride, fully planning to get a hotel room for her and Daniel, Cathy acknowledged aloud, "This is going to be too expensive of a trip to do regularly. But Lord, are there any options?"

Instantly, Cathy saw in her mind her cousin and husband who lived a short distance from the pickup and drop-off point from her ex-husband's home.

"Wow! Was that You, Lord? I will contact them!"

At the rest stop Cathy looked their number up and called. They chatted a few minutes until she asked, "Look. I'm coming in now to pick up Daniel for my visitation... and we haven't seen you all for a while. Well, I realize this is short notice, but I was just wondering if you would like us to visit?"

Immediately her cousin insisted that they come and stay with them.

"Are you sure we're not putting you out? You don't have other plans?"

The encouragement was incredible. Nancy, her cousin replied, "With the kids grown and out of town, it's just the two of us in this big ol' house! We're excited to get to see you both!"

There was a few minutes that Cathy could hear a muffled conversation going on between Nancy and her husband. A tad breathless, Nancy came back on the phone and said, "... and we *both* hope you will consider staying with us every time you get him for visitation!"

Cathy whispered, *"Thank You, Jesus!"* They chatted about sleeping arrangements and dinner preferences, with estimated time of arrival and duration of their visit. The conversation ended with, "I love you, Cuz!"

Once back in the car, Cathy remembered and recited a portion of a passage, "... and we know that God causes everything to work together for the good of those who love God..."[4] She beamed while she shouted aloud, "Thank You, Lord, for answering my prayers!"

As a mirror to Matthew 5:44, she prayerfully vowed, "I strive to learn to love my enemies, to bless those who curse me, and to do good to those who hate me." She continued, "I even pray for that man who ran me off from my home, took my child away from me, and stole years-worth of sentimental treasures acquired from my loving relatives and siblings." She prayed, "I give it all to You, Lord, I cast all of my cares on You! I pray that someday this man, Frank, who has been my enemy, will change."

Cathy prayed a prayer that would be sent up to Heaven on a regular basis for years to come:

"Dear Lord,

If only this man knew that the spiritual law of sowing and reaping is true, he would not have done these things. If only he realized that when we make evil choices, we will have consequences to face. If only he knew that heaven and hell are real, he would repent from his evil ways.

So therefore, I can truly say Lord, just as Jesus had prayed while suffering during His crucifixion, Dear Father, forgive him, for he doesn't know what he has done...[5]

In Jesus' name, amen!"

Have you ever urgently waited for answered prayer, and then received it during what you saw as at the last moment? In reality, the answer was right on time, wasn't it? God's timing is perfect! Often, in such a circumstance we have the opportunity (whether appreciated or not) to learn about patient faith; while we lean on the Lord, the answer is on the way.

Have you been able to pray for your enemy? Maybe it's even a person who intentionally, maliciously mistreated you? Was violence involved? Have you been able to see their commission of sin with the merciful eyes of Jesus?

What's the rest of this story? Here are three options, with a fourth for you to make up — you choose!

Option 1

During the three years that Cathy's visitation remained every other long weekend with Daniel, she would drive the distance alone, or her husband would come with her. They would either stay at her cousin's house or at another relative's home nearby. Their relationship grew closer to each other and with Daniel, regardless of the circumstances.

Knowing that Daniel had already experienced grave emotional trauma by being in a toxic environment while living with Frank, the effects a child suffers from their parent's divorce, and the fact that he had apparently attempted suicide at such a tender age, Cathy ensured he received counseling regularly during their visitation.

Meanwhile, Frank remarried to a woman who already had children of her own.

Over time, he and his new wife were not as disagreeable to the idea for Cathy and her husband to gain full custody. Besides, Frank's new marriage remained unpredictable and sometimes volatile.

When court date arrived, Cathy and her husband were granted custody. They took Daniel to a stable, peaceful home where he thrived in every area: academics, sports, relationships, spiritually, and his attitude improved greatly. Daniel dedicated his life to the Lord, and later went into the ministry to help youth coming from broken homes.

Did Frank change? Unfortunately, many years later, when the opportunity arrived, he successfully chased another woman from her home.

Option 2

Even though Cathy's marriage was good and appeared to be thriving, she continued to suffer from the separation from Daniel. After only a few years, her husband suddenly died, and Cathy again allowed herself to be distracted by the world while she searched for her happiness in the arms of another violent man.

As is all too often the case, Cathy found herself a man who was not so different from Frank. This man was obsessive in controlling her time; he did not like her spending visitation with Daniel. As the jealousy and possessiveness continued, the relationship with Daniel became strained. Eventually, the visitation became too emotionally difficult to continue, and that precious time with Daniel was lost, leaving both Cathy and her son feeling trapped, alone, and unloved.

As Daniel grew into adulthood, he began to act out aggressively with girlfriends, even though he abhorred his father's attitude and actions toward women. He repeatedly failed at relationships. Daniel began taking drugs to bring himself emotional relief from the conflicts within.

Meanwhile, Frank continued his pattern of abuse in his home. His actions were always ignored, excused, rationalized, or encouraged by his friends and family.

Option 3

Early in their marriage, Cathy and her new husband dedicated themselves to the Lord, and with each visit, they included Daniel in exposure to the church, shared prayers with him, and encouraged him to turn to the Lord himself. He, too, dedicated his life to the Lord.

As a united family unit, God was their primary focus. They continued to pray for and influence family members, friends, and even their enemies (even Frank). They began to see change in others and prayers being answered. Because of his age, Daniel was able to tell the court that he wanted to live with his mother and step-father in a stable home, and the custody decision was reversed.

Within a few years of this, Frank's family and Cathy's family were all actively worshiping the Lord together as God's children. They even joined each other for holidays and birthdays. All the past anger and negativity had been replaced with love, a love that only can come from the Lord.

Cathy, her new husband, and Daniel participated in many church outreach and missions programs.

Option 4

How would you end this story? Write!

THINGS TO PONDER

As you read this story about a domestic violence situation, could you see the choices each individual made along the way and the consequences they faced? Regardless of what they did, there was always a remedy: to turn to the Lord for rescue, redemption, and for salvation.

The scenarios are all too real! Do you know of a family experiencing a similar legacy of abuse? Are you part of one? What can you say or do to evoke change? Prayer is always the first thing you can do, sometimes it's the only thing you can do. With the faith of a mustard seed, you can move a mountain; you can see answered prayer!

In this story, Cathy must travel through some years of rough patches in life to get to where she should be. Some of her struggle may have been consequences as a result of her own bad choices. But, maybe sometimes we just don't know a reason why we struggle through hard circumstances. Our lives on Earth are temporary; and in that, sometimes good things can happen to bad people, and bad things can happen to good people, and we don't always get an understanding of why. Regardless, we can always turn to the Lord in prayer, praise, and patient faith. We have the opportunity to put on the full armor of God and to stand through the storm.

I hope this story influenced you to ask yourself what you can do for your future generations. I encourage you to seriously ask yourself, "What will be my legacy?"

FIVE

HOW DOES A WARRIOR PRAY?
LEARNING HOW TO FIGHT SPIRITUAL BATTLES

KARA CAREFULLY WALKED up the steep steps, holding the railing tightly to maintain her balance on this damp, dark, and dreary evening. She had searched the car, but her flashlight could not be found.

No matter, Kara assured herself, since the front porch lamp gave sufficient lighting to her path. This reminded her of a scripture, which she recited: "Your word is a lamp for my feet, a light on my path..."[1]

Kara made a last-minute adjustment to secure her face mask and reached for the door. Before she could grab the doorknob, Alane, the leader of the group, had the door open and greeted her. Kara smiled, knowing that Alane was consistently cheery and welcoming, God's excellent choice to manage the Women's Prayer Warriors group, a small satellite of their non-denominational church.

"Hello, Kara," Alane said enthusiastically, as she arm-bumped with Kara. "We have everything ready." She waited for Kara to enter before she continued, "Come help me set up the dining table."

Kara mentioned, "I appreciated that you called each of us ahead with the question, 'Have you been exposed to someone who has had the virus or tested positive?' I also appreciate your sign about it that you have taped on the screen at the front door."

Alane responded, "Yes, reminders are good; and unfortunately, this is apparently our new normal process."

Kara responded, "Well, I see you're not wearing a mask...should I wear my face mask or not?"

Alane quickly assured her, saying, "I'm leaving that up to each person. We will be able to sit far enough apart, and anyone concerned can sit separately or simply wear a mask."

"Well, most everyone has had at least one vaccine shot by now," Kara replied while she removed her mask. "I believe I'm fine." She then took off her jacket. "It's a tad chilly tonight. I guess fall weather is already here."

"Oh, yes," replied Alane. "Here, let me have your jacket." She hung it in the coat closet.

Alane took Kara for a quick tour of the kitchen area so she could see the light refreshments available thus far for the buffet-style meal.

"Wow, Alane," Kara said, nodding gratitude to the group's host, "this is really nice."

Kara helped carry items to the dining area: a bowl of grapes, a tin of crackers, and a plate of cheese. Meanwhile, Alane brought in a large pitcher of iced tea.

Alane laughed. "Since you are the first to arrive, you choose your seat. Do you want to sit near the mantle on the ottoman, on one of the sofas, or would you rather a chair?"

Kara sat on the ottoman first. "Um. Maybe a chair would actually be better for back support."

"Absolutely, Kara. And how is your back doing, by the way?"

"Oh, it's fine! But it really likes a hard chair against it. You know, it's been nearly a year since the surgery and it is healing nicely!"

"Praise the Lord! Your healing is a miracle! Do you realize how many people have gone through major back surgery only to find that they are not much better afterward? Some have remained in debilitating pain."

"I know!" Kara exclaimed. "Every day I am so grateful that He has blessed me in this way, and I pray for other people's healing."

As women arrived, they dropped off their meal contribution onto the dining table. Only Sandra, the new member, opted to keep her mask on while the women mingled in the dining area. Kara and Alane took women's jackets and coats to the closet and brought out more chairs.

Most of the ten group members (including Sandra) had arrived and began coming into the living room. They each greeted those who were already there and then selected where to sit, leaving two empty chairs still available.

Once all of the women had found seats in the living room, Alane stood in front of the group and announced, "I just want to re-emphasize a few social distancing considerations in case any of you have virus concerns before we begin... I have had the full vaccine, and I know several of you have, too. The rest have had the first of a two-part vaccine. Regardless, I think I have the seats far enough apart for your safety. It is up to each of you whether you wear a face mask or not while you are seated. Wearing a mask here at all is up to you. Are there any questions?"

She looked around the room and seeing nobody had a concern, she began their meeting.

"As all of you know, I facilitate this monthly group called the Women's Prayer Warriors, also known as 'WPW.' As most of us know, this group is comprised of women who love the Lord. Some of us have escaped various life struggles, and we all face challenges now. Regardless of our current circumstances, we each stand in prayer for our families and the community in hopes to make a difference through prayer."

She glanced around the room and stopped her gaze at their new member.

"Sandra, here," Alane emphasized, pointing to Sandra, who in turn smiled while she removed her mask. Sandra nodded to the rest of the ladies. "She is new to our group, so we can each share with her who we are and what we're up to right now."

Alane then informally announced their group mission, stating, "As I indicated previously, we gather together at least monthly to share our concerns for family members, friends, neighbors, and the community; then, we pray for them all, in agreement, knowing that when two or three are gathered together in Jesus' name, there He is in the midst of us. That's found in Matthew 18:20. We believe Jesus is actually praying with us, and for us."

Alane smiled at her audience. "Before we get started, let us begin with an opening prayer."

Barb interrupted, asking "Are we going to wait for Clara and Janice?"

Alane responded, "No, they each called to indicate that they can't make it this time. There will only be eight of us for today."

Barb nodded that she understood, and acknowledged, "Okay."

The group of women stood to their feet. Kara volunteered to say a short opening prayer:

"Dear Almighty God of all living things, King of the Universe, we are humbled before You today, and so very thankful for everything You've given us. Thank You for bringing us together today and let us always be productive toward Your Kingdom whenever the opportunity comes. We praise You with gratitude for our health and healing, for our families, and especially for Jesus' sacrifice and resurrection so that we can all enjoy an eternity with You. In Jesus' name, amen."

A chorus of "amen" was said by various women, and they all sat down at their seats.

Alane glanced at each woman. She knew them all: some from six months to two years of previous meetings and some from many years of working with them in various church programs, missions, or outreach efforts.

"Now, like I indicated earlier, let's go around the room welcoming our new member, Sandra, and she will then introduce herself to the group."

Sandra nodded and smiled in appreciation.

Alane grinned at Sandra, saying, "I am a retired history teacher; I taught high school students for twenty years at various schools within Virginia. Then, with my husband and church family's support, we began a local faith-based non-profit to benefit low-income families and community needs generally. It was brought to my attention a few years ago now that our church needed a women's group such as this to regularly pray for needs of the church family and beyond. So, here we are."

Kara, sitting beside Alane, picked up from there and said, "Hi, I know Alane from church and various outreaches we've done, and I joined this group last year." She stopped for a few seconds to smile at Sandra. "I'm retired from the Commonwealth of Virginia, where I served for thirty years in accounting, auditing, and risk management. I was saved while I was a young wife and mother, but I allowed the distractions of this world to draw me away. After wandering in the desert for forty years..." She laughed with some of the women who knew her story, then continued, "Some of it was within dangerous domestic violence situations. Finally, I rededicated my life to the Lord and He changed me! I am an author and sometimes I speak at events geared toward overcoming challenges as a domestic violence victim advocate and survivor. My favorite scripture is Psalm 34:18 in the New International Version, or NIV, 'The Lord is close to the broken-hearted and saves those who are crushed in spirit.'"

Alane responded to Kara, "Many of us can relate to your wandering in the wilderness for forty years, like the Israelites. It is scary how easily we can lose our focus on the Lord and let the distractions of the world grab ahold of us. Thank you, Jesus, for bringing Kara back, and each of us back into the fold."

Alane then focused directly on Sandra and explained, "You'll find that many of us in this group are domestic violence victim advocates and some are survivors. But we have concern and interest in other serious social issues as well, such as human trafficking and elder abuse...we love all people and want the best for everyone."

Lydia, a lovely human trafficking victim advocate who had worked with Kara and Alane in outreach programs a few times, quickly introduced herself next.

"I'm a retired military officer who also suffered from domestic violence. Now. I am a leader in a non-profit that offers annual scholarships for women who have come from a violence arena, whether from human trafficking, sexual abuse, or domestic violence." She scratched her head and added, "I think I'll share my favorite scripture, like Kara did. Mine is Proverbs 14:31, 'Whoever oppresses a poor man insults his Maker, but he who is generous to the needy honors Him.'" [2]

Gracie smiled at Lydia and then shared that she currently works on the product line for Amazon at the local warehouse.

"My initial interest in joining this group was because some of the group members here, especially Alane, reached out to me when my husband died. I was in terrible pain from the grief and at the lowest point in my life. I felt alone. With the love and help from these women, I know that the Lord is always with me, and I am certainly never alone." Gracie added, "I learned that although my grieving period was overwhelming, I was not alone, and it would not last forever. My favorite scripture is: '...Weeping may stay for the night, but rejoicing comes in the morning.' That's in Psalm 30:5."[3]

Valorie cleared her throat and said, "Sandra, we're so happy to have you join us! I am a work-from-home mom, and I'm on the internet selling goods when not busy with the kids and my husband. I love my life. It's hard to imagine that I once was a drug addict living on the streets while I was a young adult. But the Lord saved me and lifted me out of that. I'm forever grateful!" She smiled at the group. "Whenever possible, I try to witness to fellow workers; but always, I try to be a shining example of the character of Jesus." She grabbed her pocket Bible from her purse beside her and turned to a book-marked page and said, "Here is my favorite Bible verse: 'Let your light shine before men in such a way that they may see your good deeds *and* moral excellence, and [recognize and honor, and] glorify your Father Who is in Heaven.'"[4]

Various women shouted in unison, "Praise the Lord!"

Barb's introduction was short.

"Hi, I'm Barb. Been with this group a few months and I really enjoy the support and prayers we have for each other. Please continue to pray for my son, who is nineteen years old and since this spring, he has been out—somewhere on the streets." She explained to Sandra, "He has been hooked on drugs and alcohol for some time, and his problems got a thousand times worse since his father suddenly died early last year — maybe it was a heart attack or COVID-19 that took him. We didn't get to say goodbye before he passed away in the hospital. We were not allowed to have a funeral at that time. It's all been really hard to deal with."

Kara spoke up, "Barb, I know what it's like to have to face the unknown regarding our loved ones." She paused, "Some of you know, but my childhood was filled with abuse in a dysfunctional family. It was found that my mother was mentally ill... anyway, while I was a teenager, she died mysteriously. There was no investigation, and we never found out for certain what had happened. Maybe it was suicide; maybe it was murder."[5]

She looked around at the group; everyone was eager to hear the rest of her story. Kara continued, "I finally came to realize that whatever happened, God is good and merciful; He is in control. If it was suicide, then I rely on God's mercy. If it was murder, I rely on the Lord's justice."

"Excellent point, Kara!" Alane emphasized, "we just need to give all our upset, problems, and the unknown's we have on earth to God, knowing what a loving Heavenly Father He is. He has a good plan, regardless of what we might see happening right now."

Lydia added, "Yes... as we face the unknown in life, we can turn to God, lean on Him, for our safety and shelter. He is our ultimate provider. We can rely on His unconditional love, goodness, and justice."

The group said "amen" in unison.

Alane added, "Thank you Kara, for sharing."

Valorie asked, "When was the last time you've heard from your son, Barb?"

"Oh, I don't know. Sometime last month he called for money, but he wouldn't say where he was. I would have considered giving him money, but he hung up before I could find out where to take it." She rubbed her temples. "It's very frustrating."

Kara promised, "We will all continue to pray for your son! The Lord is working with him right now. You need to give it to the Lord and leave all the hard stuff for Him to handle." She watched Barb sadly shaking her head, and continued speaking to her with a more compassionate, softer tone. "I know that was easy for me to say. But in reality, you may need to turn to God repeatedly when those stressful thoughts come to you."

The other members of the group nodded in agreement.

Barb explained, "That's how it is with me. I pray, I give it to God, and then in a little while my worries and fears come back."

"Oh, yes," Alane agreed, knowingly, "that's because a spiritual enemy is whispering to you, enticing you to return to dark, negative, and scary thoughts. But God has a good plan working right now for your son."

Lydia chimed in, "You are facing spiritual warfare! That evil force, or the Devil, wants you to be devastated, to lose faith that better things are ahead for you and your son." She glanced around at the other members, cueing them to join her.

All of the older members shouted their jingle together, saying, "WPW, fight, fight, fight! We keep praying while God keeps listening! Answered prayers are on the way!"

Everyone excitedly clapped their hands.

Sandra gazed at the group with wide-eyed surprise. Gracie whispered to her, "That's our mantra. We say it at least once every meeting." Sandra smiled while Gracie added, "An excellent reminder to have patient faith in the Lord."

Sandra nodded her head in agreement.

Tracy was the last to introduce herself to Sandra, but before she had the opportunity to speak, Alane interrupted.

"Sorry, Tracy, but before we go further, let's take a minute to tell Sandra what we mean when we say our mantra..."

Gracie explained, "To me, it emphasizes that God is the one who fights our battles for us, when we turn to Him with patient faith. And when we keep that faith and trust while we wait, we can hope to see our prayers answered."

Kara began to read out loud, "'The LORD will fight for you, and you shall hold your peace.'" She looked up from her Bible. "That's Exodus 14:14 in the New King James Version."

Alane said to Sandra, "You may notice that we turn to the Word of God often. We do that on purpose — after all, it is our only weapon against the enemy, the Devil. The word of God is referred to as the sword of the spirit in Ephesians 6:17." She then looked around and asked, "Anyone else?"

Valorie raised her hand for a second, held up her iPhone and read aloud, "And this is the confidence that we have toward Him, that if we ask anything according to His will, He hears us. And if we know that He hears us in whatever we ask, we know that we have the requests that we have asked of Him."[6]

Immediately after Valorie finished, Barb recited, "Cast your burden on the LORD, and He will sustain you; He will never permit the righteous to be moved."[7]

Alane joined in, "This is one of my favorites "Let us then with confidence draw near to the throne of grace, that we may receive mercy and find grace to help in time of need.'"[8]

Alane tapped her temple and realized that Tracy had not yet had her turn speaking. She announced to the group, "Oops, hold it..." She explained to Sandra, "We have one more person to introduce herself to you, Tracy."

Alane motioned toward Tracy with her hand.

Tracy proceeded, "Hi, Sandra, we're all glad that you could come join us! I'm Tracy, part-time grocery cashier and currently living alone in an apartment complex in a rough part of town—I'm hoping to move to something better soon. My family is grown and gone, so it's just me. I've been with the group about six months and love them all." She cleared her throat, smiling, and then she continued, "I like what it says in Joshua 1:9: 'This is My command — be strong and courageous! Do not be afraid or discouraged. For the Lord your God is with you wherever you go.'"[9]

Valorie shouted, "Yes, we are strong women! The Lord is with us!"

Others shouted in unison, "Amen, sister!"

Finally, it was Sandra's turn. She timidly began her story.

"Well, I'm a new Christian — been with the church only a month or so... I'm guessing we all go to the same church?" She gazed around the circle of new friends, and they each gave an encouraging nod. "Anyway, it was suggested that I join this group, for a number of reasons..."

Sandra began to wring the tissue in her hand, stifling her emotions.

"My sister-in-law just died from COVID-19, and my brother is now in the hospital in New York." A single tear ran down her face and she wiped it away. "It's so heartbreaking because she and I, well, we were close. I loved her like a sister, and now she is gone. And, like you, Barb," she said, nodding her head at Barb, "we didn't get to have a funeral for her, and I have dreams about her all the time."

Sandra blew her nose into the tissue and balled it up. She straightened in her chair and composed herself.

"And now, the family can't see my brother, although we're being told he is progressing... and he is not on a ventilator..." She looked down at her tissue and glanced back at the women. "Life just seems tough right now."

Sandra tried to stifle her emotions, but the tears began to fall. The other women automatically put their masks back on (out of respect for her) and gathered around her in prayer.

Several women had a hand or both hands on Sandra's shoulders, and the women in the back had their hands on the ones in front, like a chain. Alane began the prayer, with others following as the Holy Spirit led them.

"Dear Heavenly Father, we know that Your love for us is unconditional and everlasting. As tragedies on Earth do come, we lean on You for help and direction. We trust that Your will shall be done in every situation; we know You are loving and just all the time; You have a good plan for us. We believe that our sufferings here on Earth may last for a little while, but joy comes in the morning; they are all temporary. Our loved ones who have passed away are now safe in Your precious arms and they are free from the pains and strife of this world.

"We might not know what is going on with Sandra's brother, but we do know that You are the one in control. We ask You, Lord, to save his soul, heal him in a mighty, supernatural way, and protect him from any harm that could come to him. Please Lord, bring him back to his family. And Lord, thanks be to You for taking Sandra and her family under Your wings of comfort and peace through their period of grief. Bless this family, Lord, in Jesus' name!"

Lydia recited, "'Heal me, O Lord, and I shall be healed; save me, and I shall be saved, for You are my praise.'"[10] Then she prayed, "Dear Lord, we lean on you to heal us completely, whether it be physically, emotionally, spiritually or financially...our hope and trust is in You. Specifically, we pray now for Sandra's brother and Barb's son, for their healing."

After a short pause, Kara prayed for Sandra, "We are grateful to You, dear Lord, for Your unconditional love, goodness and peace. We ask You to overwhelm Sandra and her family now with Your supernatural healing and compassion. We ask that for each of us and our families, as well as our church family and the community, whatever those needs may be. In Jesus' name..."

After several individuals prayed, one by one, the women went back to their seats. After they had returned to their seats, Barb made a kind offer to Sandra.

"Sandra, it appears that you and I are in the same type of worries and concerns right now, grieving while we're facing the unknown with my son missing and your brother in the hospital. Would you like to be my prayer partner? We could lift up our loved ones to the Lord together. We can set up a day and time to pray regularly. How does that sound?"

"Oh, yes, I would love that," Sandra quickly agreed.

Tracy said, "That's what Gracie and I do early every morning."

"Yes," chimed in Gracie, "and I love our prayer time together. We know that our prayers are more powerful when done in unity and agreement with another believer."

"Amen," commented Valorie. "My husband and I pray together every evening."

Alane looked at the clock on the wall, noticing their time was getting away from them. She announced to the group, "Let's all proceed to the dining area for our dinner, buffet-style. After you have filled your plate, gathered utensils and drink, please go sit where you may feel comfortable. There should be plenty of room to spread out within the dining and living room areas to meet any virus-related concerns."

The women proceeded to form a line to the dining room table. Once each had selected their seats with full plates, the women engaged in light conversation and laughter while they ate.

Lydia announced, "As usual, Tracy has brought a delicious dessert!"

Barb laughingly said, "Tracy, you're blowing my diet, but I love you for bringing this!"

Tracy answered, "The chocolate pudding is sugar free, so eat all you want!"

Each of the women complimented and thanked each other for the food brought and they expressed gratitude to Alane for being the hostess.

After everyone had finished with their meal, Sandra replaced her face mask and they returned to the living room. Alane asked for any specific prayer requests, with the intention of continued prayer until their next meeting.

Barb said, "Just a reminder, please continue prayers for my family's healing over the loss of my husband, and that my son will be miraculously healed from his addictions and come safely home."

Valorie added, "Amen, with God all things are possible. If He lifted me out of my addictions, He can certainly bring your son out of it and back home!"

Gracie cleared her throat, "I have a special request today. I don't think I've mentioned anything about a friend of mine before. Her name is Mona, and I'm seriously concerned about her." She looked around the group and noted that all of the women were watching her and listening intently.

"Mona is in her eighties now, retired, and has up till recently, enjoyed living independently in her home. What happened was this: one evening two months ago now, while Mona was alone, she fell. She was on the floor all night. To this day, Mona does not know whether she had passed out and then fell to the floor or passed out because she tripped and fell. Her memory of exactly what happened is not there. She did come to during the night, but she was in a lot of pain and her leg was injured, so she decided not to try to get up, knowing that her daughter would be there early in the morning. So then, Mona's daughter found her on the floor."

Lydia asked, "Is she alright now?"

Gracie nodded her head and continued, "Yes, she did go to the hospital, spent some time in rehab and all that, and now her leg is nearly healed one-hundred percent." She looked at her hands and shook her head. "But the thing is, because of her accident while alone, and because she doesn't know what brought on that fall — whether she tripped and fell or just passed out, causing her accident, this is the bottom line: Mona is not allowed to live alone anymore."

This news upset the group.

Alane asked, "What do you mean, she can't live alone in her home any longer? Who is saying this?"

Gracie confirmed, "At first, she was allowed to have her grandson staying with her at her house. But that setup quickly became a problem with her grandson's busy schedule. So, her family moved her in with her daughter."

The group of women sheepishly looked at each other, knowing this could have happened to any of them. Kara asked, "Is that working out for her? Sometimes it turns out well...after an adjustment period..."

"No, it's not so great." Gracie sadly shared, "Mona and her son-in-law never really got along. There is always an undercurrent of animosity and her daughter is typically the bossy type. Anyway, I went to see her the other day. to see if she needed me to get anything for her."

A tear rolled down Gracie's face and she dabbed her eyes with a tissue.

"While I was there Mona whispered to me why she couldn't stand it there. They expected her to sit parked and strapped in a wheelchair, watching television all day. The only reason she needs a wheelchair, mind you, is because they decided she needs it when they are not in the room. Yes, I know — they don't want her to fall again. She realizes the family is busy, but still, she feels like a piece of forgotten furniture thrown into the corner." Gracie wrung her hands. "It's hard enough for her, to suddenly lose her independence, and not to be around her own things...I felt so sorry for her! But there is nothing I can do." She paused. "Am I right, or is there something I can do?"

Alarmed at what she had just heard, Tracy asked the group, "Who has the authority to take her from her home like that? Is it because she had given her daughter power of attorney? Or was this initiated by her doctor, for her own safety?"

Alane said, "Well, what else could have been done? Maybe that was the only quick fix they could think of under the circumstances. Adjusting to a retirement facility might be hard, too."

Barb suggested, "Gracie, if you're up to it, I encourage you to continue to see her often while she's trying to adjust to this major transition. You know, to keep her spirits up... and you can be like her 'wellness check' at the same time."

Gracie put up her hands, resigning to what she could or could not do. "I'm not sure how that will work, but I'll try. I got the feeling

Mona is on a tight leash. Her daughter gave me a specific time I could visit and came back into the room within an hour."

Lydia offered, "Well, from what we've heard so far, it doesn't sound like an immediate danger, so I would not advise calling the police or the elder abuse hotline.[11] But if you suspect she is being mistreated in any way, I think I'd start with contacting the local adult protective services for information."

Valorie added, "I think if doctors or home health providers are suspicious of abuse or neglect, then they're mandated to report it."

"Really, Valorie?" Tracy wondered out loud, "Where did you get that information?"

Valorie's face turned red with embarrassment and she admitted, "Well, I think I saw it on a Dr. Phil show. We might want to check out that little fact..."

Lydia determined, "Let's pray about it today. Before our next meeting, I'll talk with a friend of mine who is a professional and deals with elder abuse issues all the time; he can supply us with good information and a hotline number to call, just in case."

Barb suddenly remembered something and exclaimed, "Oh, I have something to add to this topic! I met with a friend I haven't seen for a few years while in the grocery store the other day. She was talking about how her family had to take her father out of his home because he could not take care of himself anymore. She was stressed with the burden of getting rid of the bulk of his belongings because he was placed into a room with another older man. I think his house is on the market now. It sounded awful to me! I mean, can you imagine being ousted from your home?"

Barb noted the shocked reactions by the other women and requested, "Lydia, maybe you could get your expert-friend to consider talking with the group sometime? We're all getting older or have family members who are elderly, so this is a topic we need to know more about."

Kara agreed, "Yes, and it wouldn't hurt for us to find out about the latest fraudulent activities and scams that are targeted toward those who are considered elderly."

Alane announced, "And, I just recently found out that age fifty is sometimes considered elderly. Did you know that?"

"Yikes!" shouted Valorie, "I didn't realize it — I'm already elderly!"

Alane asked, "Does anyone else have something for us to pray about before we have a closing prayer? It can be an unspecified prayer request, meaning the specific details need only be known by you and the Lord…"

Lydia squirmed in her seat for a minute, then pushed herself to reveal her suspicions. She blurted, "I don't know what's going on, really, but I have a family in my neighborhood that seems to have odd activities going on. So, I just want us to pray for them, especially for the kids."

This piqued everyone's interest.

Alane asked, "Like what? What are they doing that's got you suspicious?"

Reluctantly, Lydia added, "It's just that the kids go somewhere every weekend, like clockwork, and then come back for school. I see them catch the school bus, but they don't ever play outside. The family seems to stay off to themselves; I mean, they have no friends that I'm aware of."

Kara offered, "The regular weekend thing may just be regular visitation with an ex-spouse of one of the parents."

Lydia agreed, "I wondered that, too. There is nothing more, really, that I can point to. Maybe I am reading too much into it since I'm involved in human trafficking victim advocacy. But sometimes that is the scenario in human trafficking: down the road it's found that the parent or guardian sends them out for the sake of drugs, money, blackmail, or whatever reason...well, my mind naturally goes there..."

"And what do they find out?" Barb asked, "What's happening with the children?"

Lydia frowned. "Sometimes they're into forced labor. Sometimes, it could be for sexual exploitation."

"Oh." Barb sadly shook her head. "Kind of sorry I asked..."

Alane turned to Lydia with encouragement, "Hey, your gut is telling you something wrong is going on there. Maybe it's the Holy Spirit prompting you?" She clasped her hands to her heart. "I say we pray for that family, even though we don't know what's going on with them."

Gracie agreed, "Amen!"

The other women nodded in agreement.

Alane announced to the group for Sandra's benefit, "We'll go around the room in prayer, like we did with our introductions. We don't need to pray eloquently or in a grandiose manner; we don't even need to pray out loud. Pray only as the Holy Spirit prompts you. This time, our meeting has been spent in much prayer already, which is a picture of praying without ceasing. Whether aloud, silently, or even if you're just remaining in a mindfulness of other people's needs, we strive to be prayerful in our relationship with the Lord.

Like in 1 Thessalonians, we strive to 'rejoice always, pray without ceasing...'"[12]

Kara reminded the group, "Always, we want to be wearing the full armor of God, so we can stand when spiritual warfare comes. As in Ephesians 6:10-20, we want to be ready, knowing what that entails." She glanced at Alane. "I'll start...

"Dear Heavenly Father, our Creator, we praise You always.

"Lord, please help us hold our thoughts captive from evil and to always maintain the believer's mindset. We know that Jesus is the way, the truth, and the life; our salvation is in Jesus. We are thankful for Your grace and all You have done for us. We strive to demonstrate our gratitude by living in obedience to Your Word and by remaining peaceful with others as much it is possible.

"We keep our faith, with the focus on You, Lord, and Your Kingdom. The Word of God is alive in us! We are filled with zeal and enthusiasm as your servants; we do good works in the unique calling each of us has received from You, always to Your glory. We are filled with faith, hope, and love in You.

"As we pray for each other's needs, and that of our families, church family, our neighbors, the community, and even for our nation and beyond, our trust is in the Lord! Your will and Your timing is perfect. We ask that You save, heal, and protect us all from evil; we pray this for those we love, for those we know, and even for our enemies. In Jesus' name!"[13]

Each woman prayed, either out loud or silently, as the Holy Spirit led them. Prayer time naturally came to an end, and they gathered their coats, said their goodbyes, and went their separate ways.

This story captures a culmination of how a community of believers may wear their full armor of God, in prevention and while the temptations and calamities come.

Within this small group of women, what do you see?

- *They follow Jesus and persevere in their Christian walk together; encouraging each other's growth.*
- *They know the strength there is in numbers as believers pray with praise and worship to the Lord.*
- *Faith, hope, and love are peacefully demonstrated as they interact with fellow believers and within the community.*
- *There is constant trust and reliance upon the Lord for answered prayers, in His timing and His way.*
- *Lovers of God read, study, and know the Word of God as they live out His word through obedience and consistent application.*
- *Each person has a unique purpose. As they serve others within their calling they are serving the Lord to His glory.*
- *They are always ready to share the good news of Jesus with gratitude, joy, and enthusiasm.*

ABOUT THE AUTHOR

Carin Jayne Casey's background is filled with life-threatening child abuse and domestic violence; then she faced abuse by toxic people. But God rescued her through it all. For that, she is forever grateful.

Casey strives to educate and encourage people to conquer life challenges. As she recovered from her own troubles, her gratitude toward the Lord motivated her to write books and to provide podcasts for others to gain tools in their overcoming process, to find victory and enjoy life.

Casey served four years on the Board of Directors for Yeshua's House (www.yeshuashouse.net), a faith-based, non-profit safe haven for women overcoming domestic violence and/or financial issues. She currently participates in various outreach efforts with local church groups.

Casey graduated from Radford University and served the Commonwealth of Virginia for thirty-one years. Carin Jayne Casey is the author's pen name.

Author. Speaker. Podcaster.
Domestic Violence Victim Advocate. Ambassador for Christ.
https://CarinJayneCasey.com
https://www.Facebook.com/Turn2GodwCarin
CarinJayneCasey - @Turn2GodwCarin on Instagram

ALSO BY CARIN JAYNE CASEY

- *A New Song Rises Up! Sharing Struggles Toward Salvation*: Christian Social Issues, Inspiration, Mental and Spiritual Healing; Casey candidly shares survival of horrible and life-threatening experiences; and yet, she presents a journey filled with forgiveness, healing, peace, deliverance, and salvation.

"...This book will walk you through the challenges we all face... She takes you through what commonly trips us up from victory and shares how to get free for the new life promised in Christ..." -- Yolanda Gray, Professional Certified Life Coach, Author, Speaker

- *My Dear Rosa Jean*: Suspense, Fiction, Christian fiction; It depicts a woman's process of overcoming domestic violence and finding victory.

"... a DV advocate whose mantra is 'Awareness. Compassion. Recovery. Peace.' It is not surprising that she has written a novel which advocates can use for public awareness, and also as a tool for those in bondage or in recovery." -- Angela Brown, Founder of Yeshua's House

"... It progressed with such intensity that it took my breath away as to how someone could not only endure these events but how they could even survive....A vivid account that left me thankful and humbled to the Grace and Mercy of God who not only is with us, but carries us through all situations." -- Loretta Thompson

- *Mystery at Candice Bay*: Mystery, Fiction, Young Adult; This is a page-turner, involving teens and their community experiencing escalating alarm as they are bombarded with unexplained events.

"... it kept me in suspense throughout the book. About the time I felt I knew who committed the crime things changed." -- Christina Buckalew

- *Granny Babysits the Mischievous Five*: Children's Chapter Book.

- *Turn to God with Carin* by Carin Jayne Casey: A weekly podcast since 2016, *Turn to God with Carin* promotes hope in healing and overcoming challenges, always sharing the Good News of Jesus. All of her video episodes are available at Carin Jayne Casey on YouTube, the related audio provided through https://buzzsprout. com/1275572, and at https://CarinJayneCasey.com.

NOTES

Who Is Directing Your Steps?

1. "Criminal Arraignment: What To Expect" by Lauren Baldwin, contributing author, criminaldefenselawyer.com.
2. The Code of Virginia, Title 18.2 Crimes and Offenses Generally, Chapter 4, Crimes against the Person, Article 1, Homicide, Section 18.2-32. First and second degree murder defined; punishment. "All murder other than capital murder and murder in the first degree is murder of the second degree and is punishable by confinement in a state correctional facility for not less than five nor more than forty years."
3. John 3:16, New International Version (NIV) (emphasis added)
4. John 4:16, New International Version (NIV) (emphasis added)
5. Excerpt from "Hope for Your Future: Do You Face Challenges You Need To Overcome?" brochure by Carin Jayne Casey, published in 2020.
6. Excerpt from "Hope for Your Future: Do You Face Challenges You Need To Overcome?" brochure by Carin Jayne Casey, published in 2020.

Which Path Will You Take?

1. Generally, information regarding trains, destinations, terminology, and locations (i.e., for a bed and breakfast and a restaurant) were found through general "google" research on the internet and on AMTRAK's site specifically.

When Will Justice Prevail?

1. Reference to Genesis 50:20 in the Amplified Bible (AMP) at a time when Joseph, the one who was in charge of dispensing all the grain in the land for Egypt and beyond during a seven-year drought, was conversing with his brothers, who had years before this encounter sold Joseph into slavery: "As for you, you meant evil against me, but God meant it for good in order to bring about this present outcome, and that many people would be kept alive [as they are this day]."
2. Mark 7: 20-23, New International Version.
3. Scriptures to support the blood of Jesus cleansing us from sin include: Matthew 26:26-28; Mark 14:22-24; Luke 22:14-20; Romans 3:25; Ephesians 2:13; Hebrews 13:12-21; 1 John 2:2; Revelations 7:14.

1 John 1:7, King James Version (KJV), (emphasis added):
"But if we walk in the light, as He is the light, we have fellowship one with another, and the blood of Jesus Christ His Son cleanseth us from all sin."

4. Concepts from scriptures: Genesis 1:26, created by God; Jeremiah 1:1-5, knew us and our purpose before the womb, Psalm 57:2, God has a purpose for each person, and Jeremiah 20:11, God's plans for us are good.

What Will Be Your Legacy?

1. 1 2 Chronicles 7:14, New Living Translation, NLT
2. 1 Corinthians 10:13, New Living Translation, NLT (emphasis added)
3. Matthew 18:20 is reference
4. Romans 8:28, New Living Translation, NLT
5. In reference to Luke 23:24, New International Version, NIV: "Jesus said, 'Father, forgive them, for they do not know what they are doing'..."

How Does A Warrior Pray?

1. Psalm 119:105, New International Version, NIV
2. Proverbs 14:21, Eastern Standard Version, ESV, emphasis added
3. Psalm 30:5, New International Version, NIV
4. Matthew 5:16, Amplified Bible, AMP
5. Further discussion into this topic is available at Carin Jayne Casey on YouTube, "Facing the Unknown," https://youtu.be/EByRdjgxKdE or Audio: https://buzzsprout.com/1275572
6. 1 John 5:14-15, Eastern Standard Version, ESV, emphasis added
7. Psalm 55:22, Eastern Standard Version, ESV, emphasis added
8. Hebrews 4:16, Eastern Standard Version, ESV
9. Joshua 1:9, New Living Translation, NLT, emphasis added
10. Jeremiah 17:14, Eastern Standard Version, ESV, emphasis added
11. References: the Virginia Elder Abuse Hotline 888-832-3858, report elder fraud 833-372-8311, the National Center on Elder Abuse, 855-500-3537, and Elder Care Locator, 800-677-1116; Human trafficking—Justicehouseofhope.org, sharedhope.org, and unstoppableyouministries.org, richmondjusticeinitiative.com. Further resources are listed at https://carinjaynecasey.com/help-and-resources
12. 1 Thessalonians 5:16-18, Eastern Standard Version, ESV
13. Prayer comes from our relationship with the Lord and knowing the Word of God. Here, a prayer may point to previous scriptures and may include: 2 Corinthians 10:5: Captive thoughts; John 14:6: Jesus is the way, the truth, and the life...; James 4:7: Submit or obey God; 2 Corinthians 13:11, Romans 12:18:

Live in peace; Colossians 3:15: Thankful with peace of Christ; Matthew 6:33: Focus on His Kingdom; 2 Timothy 3:16-17: Word of God or all scripture is God breathed; 1 Corinthians 13:13: Faith, hope, and love; Romans 12:11: Serve Him with enthusiasm or zealously; Mark 12:28-31: Pray for love; Matthew 5:45-48, Love your enemies; John 14, 16: Pray in Jesus' name

CPSIA information can be obtained
at www.ICGtesting.com
Printed in the USA
BVHW081004280521
608375BV00002B/172

9 781950 306862